GW00401762

THIS WAS OUR VILLAGE

Kathleen Stratford

First published in 2010 by Kathleen Stratford
Copyright © Kathleen Stratford 2009

ISBN 978-0-9563157-0-0

The right of Kathleen Stratford to be identified as the
Author of this work has been asserted by her in accordance
with the Copyright, Designs and Patents Act 1988.

All rights reserved. No part of this publication may be
reproduced, stored in a retrieval system, or transmitted,
in any form or by any means without the prior written
permission of the publisher.

Although the stories contained in this publication are based
upon the experiences of the Author during her early life,
all characters are fictitious and any resemblance to a real
person, living or dead, is purely coincidental.

Book designed by Paul Stratford and
typeset by Michael Walsh at
THE BETTER BOOK COMPANY
5 Lime Close Chichester PO19 6SW

Printed and bound by
ASHFORD COLOUR PRESS
Unit 600 Fareham Reach
Fareham Road
Gosport
Hants PO13 0FW

To My Sons Paul and Ian

CONTENTS

ACKNOWLEDGEMENTS

My grateful thanks to everyone who encouraged me in this venture, particularly my sons who helped prepare the book and its cover for publishing.

Also thanks to Peggie for the graphics.

THIS WAS OUR VILLAGE

Introduction

Our village was just a tucked-away place, nestling at the foot of the Berkshire Downs.

High along its back ran the centuries-old Ridgeway, cart-tracked and grass covered, but still used by the shepherds and farmers.

To find the village you would have to turn off the turnpike road on to the narrow one bordered by meadows and an orchard, and that divided itself into long winding streets, and like the spokes of a wheel linked up again at the crossroads by the church.

This quiet little backwater was once a hive of activity during the high days of the woollen trade, when fleeces were brought long distances by pack horses; the wool, we were told, was washed and dried on the grass slopes in the village, then bagged and taken to the markets for auction.

Thatched cottages, mostly of black and white daub, kept company with a grand Georgian-fronted mansion, a Tudor house partly converted into a shop, and an old manor sheltered behind a red-bricked wall. On the bank stood a chapel that had been closed and fenced in for years, the windows barred and the door heavily padlocked. Some said that a secret passage led to the 'Big House', and had been used by the monks during the 'persecution'.

Squire's widow's house was there, right in the heart of the village; grey-stoned and imposing with its private chapel. Surrounding it lawns, and leading to the main door a sand-covered driveway edged with clipped yew trees and hedges; everywhere speaking of former prosperity.

The church with its Norman arches and fine carving inside, had an ancient wooden clock perched up in the belfry, and which played part of a hymn at each quarter hour and the full version on the hour. Years ago this place of worship had been used by the Catholics, the late Squire's ancestors were all buried in the side chapel, the walls covered in marble scrolls, testimonials of their worth, as a reminder to the community. Times changed, the Catholics had a new church built for themselves on a hill very close to the 'Big House', and when the sound of bells floated over the village on a Sunday from the old church it called Parson and only the Protestants.

Not too far from the turnpike road stood an old hostelry, inviting weary travellers to "Come, stop and spend a social hour," in an amusing sign on the front of the building. Two other inns served the public, one bearing the late Squire's coat of arms on its creaking signboard, and the other was known as 'spit-and-sawdust' by the locals, and had a large spittoon on a floor strewn with sawdust in the public room.

Tradesmen there were a-plenty, scattered around the village: builder, wheelwright, and carpenter, blacksmith, shoe-repairer, dressmaker and nurse, butcher, baker, and two grocers. All catered for our needs; we needed only to go outside the village for our outings. Of course, the wool sorters and the baggers had gone long ago, their descendants now mainly agricultural workers, and the employers now Squire's widow, a corn farmer, and a rich man who called himself a 'Gentleman Farmer'. The latter believed in hygiene, order and progress, and was viewed with grave suspicion by his workers, "'ee made us white wash the pigsty and the 'en 'ouse, that 'ee did," they shook their heads in despair at such waste of time.

There was a strict social ladder in the village during the period of my growing up (from 1914). The end of the First World War would see the breaking up of the social structure, but the pace was slow and by 1930, when I left home for good, things were much the same as they had always been. We had the 'Nobs', such as Squire's widow and her children, next the 'Gentleman Farmer', several Majors and a local magistrate. Down the ladder to the artist and his wife, two retired singers, a writer, priest, Parson and his wife, and a Wesleyan minister. Several rungs down came the dressmaker, nurse and tradesmen, and, so we were told, on the bottom rung were the labourers.

All worked hard to see that the positions were kept, all excepting our lady at the top and her family; they could at least boast of a famous ancestor who had spoken plainly to a King and was beheaded for sticking to his principles.

So to this village in 1913 came my parents, my father having secured a post as chauffeur to the 'Gentleman Farmer', and the car that he drove was one of the first to be seen in the village and caused quite a stir, to say nothing of Dad in his special uniform and peaked cap. A cottage went with the job, and my family lived in it for over forty years, until they died and were buried in the cemetery on the hill, along with their friends who'd once called them 'foreigners'.

THIS WAS OUR VILLAGE

Chapter One

THE BEGINNING

November 1914 saw that winter the worst weather the village had ever seen, not that I was aware of either event, for with Ma's help I was making an appearance into this world.

Three years of growing up must have not soaked in to my head, for the only thing I can clearly recall to this day is the moment I first met my father.

I remember waking up in a big feather bed, and hearing soft thudding noises at the bedroom window, Ma sat bolt upright beside me, listened for a second, then flung all the bedclothes back, letting in cold air. Feet paddled across the room and the sash cord was pulled hard.

"Who's there?" she called out into the black night.

"It's me," came a loud deep voice from below the window.

Ma's head and shoulders re-appeared, and she hastily put a coat over her nightie.

"That's your Dad" I heard as matches were struck and a thin light transferred to the candle, "Home on leave, at last." She hugged me tight and bustled down the stairs to let him in.

Sleep left me, I sat up and thought about this man, who Ma seemed to like very much but I'd never seen, my feet making long lines in the warm feather mattress, whilst I tried to decide what being "on leave" meant.

Down below came the sound of coal being

heaped into the grate, and the kettle lid that just wouldn't sit still, then later the smell of fried bacon, they must be having breakfast and forgotten me – well – I'd go and tell them I was hungry too.

By the table in the kitchen, sat a thin man in a jacket that had gold-coloured buttons all down the front of it, he was reading out loud to my mother from a piece of paper, taken from his pocket and held close to the lamp. Then I noticed the pipe he'd been smoking, stood now on Ma's best brass tray, and watched the smoke from it curl in rings up to the ceiling.

Turning, he saw me, I was picked up and squeezed very tight, kissed several times, leaving damp patches on my cheeks.

"There now, isn't your Dad nice?" Ma asked as my feet touched the floor again, but I wasn't so sure, and spent the rest of the evening taking little looks at him from the safety of her lap.

＊＊＊＊＊

The following year the war came to an end, and my brother brought a present home from school that he'd been given to mark the occasion. It was a cream-coloured mug with two painted figures on one side – Ma said they were pictures of our King and Queen – and the gold lettering along the bottom "1914-1918."

A few days later we had the 'Peace Celebrations', when all the village turned out to enjoy themselves, and in the evening, just before it got dark, I was dressed up to ride in the procession of decorated waggons that would take us to Squire's park for the bonfire and fireworks.

White button boots, a lace dress with ribbon bows, my hair curly after being treated with rag bobbles, and funny feelings in my stomach as Ma handed me over to some older girls, who had umpteen other children they were looking after, at their heels.

Off we went, up the long street that led to the meadow, I had to run to keep up with the small ones.

"Come on," someone said, "let's give thee a piggy back, or else, damn me, 'twill be over 'fore we get there."

Jogged up and down on the broad back of a girl in plaits, we at last reached the grass field, at the far end stood empty waggons, decorated with streamers and Union Jacks. Men and boys, some carrying lanterns, moved round the horses, making sure all the straps had been properly fastened.

The girl stopped and bent over, I slid to the ground and holding hands we all raced across the meadow, to join crowds of children pushing and shoving as each tried to be first on the waggon.

I was helped on and told to "hold tight" by a youth who the girls called "one of they carters." Horses tossed their heads and showed manes tied with ribbon braids, brasses shone on leather straps as light from the flickering lanterns passed over them.

Voices seemed to be everywhere, and it was quite dark before I heard, "Come on Betsy, gee up Dobbin," and felt the loaded waggon start to move and the dull thud of horses feet on the grass.

Slowly through the village the procession came, meeting cheers from the crowds lining the long drive up to the park, and as we came to a halt by the side of the bonfire – never had I seen such a large one – thick tongues of flame seemed to reach the sky, smoke billowed out, like huge black sails.

"'Ang on, 'ang on," a carter yelled out,

as he let the board at the back of the waggon down, and children rushed past him.

"You 'old on 'ere a minute, while I finds thee Mam," my friend with the plaits said, and vanished, leaving me standing close by a pile of faggots.

Just at that moment a crowd came along, in the centre was a man rolling a barrel, and with laughs, shouts and heaves, it was hauled up and fixed firmly on top of a trestle table. I watched whilst the tap on the barrel was turned, and glasses filled with brown-coloured water that had soap suds on top but no-one seemed to mind, they just drank it down quickly and handed the glass back for another helping.

There was "swish," and a ball of light shot into the air, turned red, blue and green as it slowly sank, then vanished, followed by bangs and smoke from way down the field. People moved across to get a better view.

Smoke and heat from the bonfire drifted on to my face. I felt thirsty and tried the stuff left behind in the glasses, liked it, turned the tap on and filled the glass again then sat leaning against the table leg, and closed my eyes.

Ma's voice woke me up, "She's soaked inside and out with beer!" the world was told, as arms shook my body like a feather pillow. It was followed by tut-tutting and scolding as women wiped me dry with table-cloths taken from an old wicker basket.

Soon all was forgotten as everyone joined hands, and walked very slowly round the bonfire. "Auld Lang Syne," they sang, at the top of their voices, as hands and arms pumped up and down, and daylight was not far off before everyone had finished, moved from the dying fire and started for home.

THIS WAS OUR VILLAGE

Chapter Two

THE PEACE YEARS

Already in my life my father, due to his absence in the army, seemed a shadowy figure, and now on his return, long bouts of illness (for he was badly gassed) and frantic searching for work meant that we saw very little of him.

At week-ends, his efforts to make us 'decent citizens,' as he called it, met with some up-hill work, but three trips to church on Sundays, silence at every meal, sitting with ram-rod backs, elbows well tucked in, made him feel better, even if it didn't seem that way to us.

Ma made up for all that discipline. She was easy-going and cheerful, and would stop everything to look at some new plant in the garden or a birds nest that we'd found, could quote poetry by the yard, and given to 'good works.'

When roused she was a demon, telling the world what she thought of it, then quickly subside to her normal happy self.

We'd move for dear life when the storm was on, returning when her tuneless singing could be heard from the house again. I loved her dearly, tantrums and all.

******

Two days after my fifth birthday I started at the Church of England School, a red-bricked three-roomed building with the headmaster's house close by.

The playground, pot-holed, gravelled in places and sloping, overlooked the old wool-drying ground and a smithy. One could hear the sound of the forge bellows, horses feet clattering on the cobbled front, and men shouting, through the drone of our lessons, whilst the strong smell of burnt hooves filtered into classrooms.

It was a cold dull day when I stood with about thirty other infants, waiting to go in. I wore my best dress, short-buttoned boots and a stomach that just wouldn't stay still though I held it.

A bell rang from a distance and a lady came out, she had white curly hair and a whistle fixed on a long string round her neck. "That's our teacher," someone told me, as the woman's smile embraced us all. Our names were called out and I joined the end of a ragged line, then the book she'd been reading from closed, "forward," came the order, and walking one behind the other, we marched up the steps into school.

The room was long, with scrubbed boards, and gray walls, cupboards ran down the length of one side, open and overflowing with papers and books, string, a teddy bear, and two black golliwogs. Close by, a round pot-bellied stove belched out heat and smoke as the wind made queer noises in the chimney.

Desks were grouped in the centre of the room and a table with stout legs stood in the corner, and on it a silver knife dug into a partly peeled apple, crayons, blotting paper, glue and a pair of scissors.

Thrown across a chair hung an almost finished rug, black edged, which I touched, it felt soft and beautiful, with a needleful of red wool thrust into a circle on the canvas.

"That will be a butterfly's eye when its finished," said teacher, leading me over to a desk shared by another girl.

Soon we were given deep wooden trays filled with sand, and a short stick like a pencil.

"Draw a daisy. Now a carrot. And we'll finish with a cat's face," said our white-haired friend.

An older girl, who was helping, sang a song about bees, I ate the cake Ma had given me whilst she finished all the verses.

The afternoon was spent making pigs with plasticine, mine got so soft I couldn't get the legs on, then we were told to fold our arms on the desk use them as a pillow for our head, and close our eyes.

It was four o'clock when they woke me up and I found school had ended, the girl who would take me home waiting whilst I struggled into my coat.

"She seemed to like it," my new friend answered to my mother's anxious questioning, as I walked past them and in to the kitchen.

"Didn't want to come home," I shouted back, nice and loud, taking a good look round, to see if Ma had bought the treat she'd promised me.

Paula,

Enjoy! And thank you for passing it on to Sarah in due course.

Regards, Ian Stratford

ianstrat2@yahoo.com

...ncakes for ...her steps to ...as she finished eating a thick slice of bread and margarine coated with brown sugar, her lips making noisy smacking sounds.

"'Ad the Salvation Army woman to our 'ouse last night, wi' a box collecting money," I heard, "told us to go wi'out summat like sugar in our tea and give the sum we would 'ave spent, to the poor. Mam soon told 'er it was we that was bloody poor."

I looked at her sharply but she was laughing softly to herself and wiping her sticky hands on the front of her dress.

We both realized that the school bell had stopped and raced down the lane, reaching the group in the playground at the same time as our teacher.

"You all know that today is Shrove Tuesday," she shouted in a ringing tone that could be heard halfway across the village. "This morning will be spent in the Lord's House, the afternoon is an annual holiday."

The older girls started to form a long row, we smaller ones pushing our way in front, the boys tailed behind us.

The teacher blew a sharp blast on a whistle and we started at a near trot for the three minute distance to the church, halting just outside the graveyard.

"When you get inside, please remember

where you are," boomed the voice from the back. "No coughing, eating sweets or changing places."

The verger opened the door and we sauntered up the aisle. My friend and I filed into the first two pews, usually reserved for the gentry, the seats had long red cushions that felt soft and warm to the touch, the hassocks (one each) had patterns in bright wool, mine had GENTLE JESUS written in gold. I lifted first one foot and then the other to see it.

The Headmaster, dressed in cassock and surplice, started to play the organ whilst a boy pumped air steadily into it.

From the vestry came the man in charge, Parson, who bowed to the alter and came close to our pew, started the service with a hymn and a prayer, then slowly walked up the steps into the pulpit, folded his hands into the sleeves of his surplice, and began.

I never heard any of the sermon, for my thoughts were with the girl and her earlier swearing, she hadn't been struck down for doing this as I'd been warned, in fact she seemed just the same; I would speak to my mother later about this.

A boy next to me coughed, he was nudged and told to "Shut up thee rattle," so he put his cap over his mouth, but small noises crept out from behind it.

Movement came from the pulpit. Parson had finished, the sound of 'ONWARD CHRISTIAN SOLDIERS' poured from the organ and we with unseemly speed returned to the door by the font. It was opened and we spilled out into the cold sullen morning.

"Halfpenny and bun day," shouted the boys as they tore through the churchyard on their way to Squire's house, the service already forgotten in their haste to be first at

22

the ceremony. We followed at a slower pace with a group of Catholics, for it was only on rare occasions that we had their company.

Soon we had reached the large circle of grass just outside the main door of the house, we could see movement inside so decided to give them a taste of what was to come. Walking in single file around the edge of the grass, hands on each other's shoulders, we chanted:

"Pit Pat the pans hot,
We're coming a-Shroving,
With the butcher up your back,
A halfpenny's better than nothing."

Squire's widow, her daughters and their friends came out and stood in the middle of the circle whilst we walked round them chanting many times in our sing-song voices.

The butler-cum-handyman appeared through the open door, a large wicker basket filled with buns hanging from one arm, and a hand clasping a bowl of halfpennies. We were all given a bun and a bright new halfpenny, thanked graciously for coming, and once again reminded the afternoon was a holiday.

"What about goin' to old Fatty's," the bold girl who swore was saying to no one in particular, throwing her bun into the air and twirling round as she caught it.

"Yeah lets," we bawled back, and like sheep followed her up the street.

An old tradesmen's bike had been leaned against the window, partly hiding boxes of sweets marked "Barretts," there were bottles of fizzy lemonade, writing paper, Wills Woodbine cigarettes, and red and white shag tobacco.

A sandy cat barred our way to the steps leading to the shop and a full-grown tabby sprawled beside some bacon and cheese on the counter.

A short stout man, dressed in black breeches and gaiters, with thick dirty boots stood watching our entry, hands slowly beating a tattoo on the grey-white apron spread over his middle. "Some on yer 'as been stealin' from this 'ere shop," he said slowly, his pale blue eyes shifting from one to the other of us.

"Now I warns yer, not to touch nothin' do yer 'ear, nothin', or else —" he left the punishment unspoken.

We showed our goodwill by holding out the halfpennies in our hands, he seemed satisfied, picked up a broom and dust rose from behind the counter.

We took lots of time looking at wine gums, liquorice-laces, sherbert packets with a gold ring at the top, gobstoppers and locust beans, and came out with six clay marbles in a green paper bag, and a large peppermint-coloured alley made of glass, well pleased with the morning and our presents.

THIS WAS OUR VILLAGE

Chapter Four

SCHOOL TIME

This morning I was standing by my desk in the lower standard for the last time, for I was ten years old and now moving into a higher standard; it was only a matter of moving into another desk, for we all shared the same room, curtained off when classes were in progress.

"You'd better watch out, old Bertie's a devil of a teacher," my friend warned me, as we both stood waiting in the playground. "Ee en't nothin' like they old Cissies that bin givin' you they lessons in the lower."

"They old Cissies" were a seventeen year old pupil teacher and a tall angular woman who wore gold rimmed glasses, and thick black stockings winter and summer. She had a fine singing voice, loved putting on shows – when she'd hold the audience spellbound with her renderings of 'Rule Britannia', and other patriotic songs.

Parents whose children had stayed 'dunces' in another class, were informed by this teacher "They're near geniuses, my dear," and when yearly fetes in the park were held, exquisite embroidery and knitting would be shown by pupils helped by this talented person.

Each week any girl who showed the least interest would be invited to her house, to sew and knit for charity, whilst her mother, a lavender-and-lace old lady, filled them to the brim with biscuits and lemonade.

Popular though she might be, inside school

hours we worked at our desks in an atmosphere
of apprehension, for lessons were conducted in
a certain way, not always approved of by
the Headmaster, and classes would come to
an abrupt halt if he appeared, to be resumed
after much argument between them in low,
hissing voices.

On the first day of the new term, with
my friend's warning about the teacher still
in my head, my legs leaping up and down in
time to 'Men of Harlech' thumped out by an
older girl on an ancient piano, I reached my
desk, and stood to attention whilst the register
was called, each child answering "Yes, Sir,"
in a toneless voice as their name was called.

Feet shuffled, there were sniffs and coughs,
and a damp sickly smell of wet clothing and
bodies, as thin beads of water collected on the
windowsills, grew in size and trickled down
the grey walls, whilst all round, an air of

gloom, misery and unwilling silence.

The Headmaster walked to the end of the class, shouted our names and pointed to the new places we were to occupy, not once looking up from the list held in his hand, or showing the least interest in us whatsoever.

I cheered up at his behavior, as I thought, how could anyone be afraid of someone who didn't even notice them, and as my seat was in the front row and he still busy with his list, I sat there and studied him for a full ten minutes.

I started from his balding head down to the highly polished brown shoes, chocolate-coloured suit and matching tie, then took the rest of the time just looking at his face, but it didn't give any idea what he'd be like.

Classes sorted out, the morning started in earnest, with hymn singing for an hour, the words written on large stiff sheets of paper hanging on the wall, the pages turned over now and then by two boys.

Bertie walked round the desks, up this way, down that, hands clasped behind his back, listening. At the end of our efforts he gave his opinion in a contemptuous and sarcastic voice; those unfortunate enough to have sung out of tune, made to stand out front and "display their talent." Never again was I to feel so wretched as on that first morning.

Despite the harsh treatment we soon learnt to sing, there were sea-shanties, rounds, love songs and marches. We read and made up small tunes, had a gramophone brought into class and heard the voices of Dame Nellie Melba, Caruso and others, mixed with scraping and hissing noises which poured out of a large round horn fixed close to the record.

Polite and reasonably orderly in school, at playtime tongues and feet were loosened. We shouted and screamed at each other, as we played hop-scotch, skipped or dug holes with our boots in the rough ground to play marbles, or held cigarette cards from a chalk line on the wall, then let go, hoping they'd drop on your friend's card and you'd be the winner.

Boys never mixed with girls although we shared the same playground, and they had their own washroom, a tin shed, which they played in when it was wet, and girls got a 'punishment' if they were caught looking over the wall at them.

On fine days we'd gather at the end of the playground, to watch the horses being shod at the smithy. The carter, having brought the animal in, would fix the reins to a large ring on the wall, the shoesmith knowing the size of the horses foot would hold the leg firmly between his knees and start taking the old shoe off.

We'd hear the pumping of bellows, and

hammering of iron on anvil but nearly always the bell would ring before the job was finished, and we'd troop back into school, to hear 'Uncle Tom's Cabin', or 'Robinson Crusoe', read to us with much changing of voice and arm waving.

Other afternoons were spent on poetry and acting. Headmaster was very fond of Shakespeare's plays, and I remember the court scene from the 'Merchant of Venice', which started the whole class laughing, when I spoke the fateful words as Portia, "Is your name Shylock?"

"No 'ten't," we heard, from a red-faced boy fed up with it all. The Headmaster stood speechless for a second, then caned the youth and pushed him outside into the yard.

Towards the end of July there was the annual prize-giving, with a visit from the School Inspector, and the eldest member of the

Church Committee, a dear old man of eighty-six, and I doubt if he ever heard our songs and certainly not our poetry, for he sat there all the time taking catnaps.

Every year our ancient friend asked everyone their name and promptly forgot it, made the same speech ending with,

"Well goodbye girls and boys, this is the last time I'll see you," his voice dropping to a sad note. He came many times more to visit us and died just before his hundredth birthday.

So the days passed, reading, writing and arithmetic, sewing, drawing and geometry, every minute crammed with learning. I returned home exhausted even though I enjoyed it, thankful my journey from school was a short one; not like some of my friends, who had a three mile tramp back over the fields, whatever the weather.

THIS WAS OUR VILLAGE

Chapter Five

PLAY TIME

If schooldays took our senses and energies, the weekends were periods of utter freedom and delight, marred only on Saturdays by being asked to clean knives, or windows, mind the youngest children, dust or sweep.

We moaned and got on with it, vowing with great fervency, that we'd "run away," or "emigrate" (a new word we'd learnt).

"When are you starting?" Ma asked us, coming into the room with a tray of cakes, "only if its this morning, you'd better get a move on, perhaps you'd like me to go upstairs and help with the packing of your bags?," she went on heartlessly.

Just at that moment there was a knock on the door, we went to the window and peered out. It was old 'Georgie' the peddler, standing on the doorstep, clothed in a putty-coloured raincoat which almost reached to his boots, making him look like a square pillar-box, thick and solid from top to toe. As the door opened he called out to us in a soft pleasant voice, his blue eyes fixing ours with a bold stare. We clustered round my mother and listened to his patter.

"Walked fifteen miles so far today," he told Ma, then unfastening the top three buttons on his coat, reached into the inside pockets, drawing out boot laces, ribbons and tape, elastic, pocket linings and skeins of darning wool, at great speed.

Bending down sideways (for that was the

only way he could manage it, with all that stuff round his middle), he opened an attaché case, crammed with needles and cottons, pins and thread, scissors and thimbles.

Ma gave her order, he measured the lace and elastic with a folding tape measure, and still keeping up a flow of conversation, cut off the lengths and handed them to her.

We heard how he'd walked to Nottingham for the lace, Birmingham for the pins, his wife's aches and pains, the death of his dog Judy, and his youth.

His tales were cut short by an invitation to a cup of tea, and we sat down at the table and continued cleaning the knives on a leather covered board, Ma and Georgie carrying on the conversation, till the church clock started to chime.

"Must be off now, and thanks for your hospitality," said the peddler, and leaning to one side, picked up the case and ambled down the path.

"Drat it," my mother sounded vexed, knowing she'd gossiped too long and would have to rush the dinner, but we with our morning jobs finished, went to the crossroads to meet Dad and get a ride on his bike.

The afternoon was ours to play in the rickyard, running round the ricks or pulling the straw about, and watch the mice quietly nibbling in a darkened corner, till we got up and scattered them with our sticks. They all made for the barn, running under the rough ragged doors, with a speed we could never catch up with.

Tired of that we 'climbed the rigging' (some elm trees close by), hugging our bodies close to the leafy branches, scarcely breathing as folks passed through the lane, their snatches of conversation coming up like murmurings on the breeze.

"Let's go and see 'Whitey'," suggested
my friend, the afternoon only half over, so
we sauntered to the workshop and peered in
through the window.

It was full of the most fascinating
gadgets, for 'Whitey' was a man of all trades,
but coffin making his specialty. He lived all
alone in a room close to his bench and always
seemed to enjoy our visits.

"Who's this coffin for?" we asked, craning
our necks to see more. He scratched his head as
though he didn't know, and invited us in to
"try it for size."

My friend got in and he put the lid on
top, holding it down for a tease, and I felt the
sweat rise on my forehead and my heart race
when told it was my turn to try.

"Good fit?" he shouted, and laughed as
he raised the lid, I got up like lightning and

rushed to the door for air.

Back home to the special tea Ma always had on Saturdays, today dried haddock and thin brown bread and butter followed by iced cake, we did justice to the spread and rewarded Ma with the washing up, whilst she got out two irons, and stood them on the hob to heat.

Slow fumbling notes from the piano next door could be heard.

"I wish he'd learn to play," was the irritable comment, as irons were lifted and tested with a drop of spit. What on earth was she grumbling about, it sounded beautiful to me, and crawling into the tiny alcove by the fireplace, I put my ear against the wall and listened to the tune.

"Yes, we have no bananas," I heard, and some jingling as the left hand was pressed hard. Some of the notes were missing but I knew the tune by heart, "Yes, we have —"

came the sound through the wall,

"No bananas," I shouted loud, the music stopped and someone thumped the wall.

"God save the King" we heard.

"Let's hope he means it," said Ma, throwing the iron back on the hob with some vigour. How unreasonable she was I thought, as I opened the front door and stood watching the jackdaws settling in the holes of the old church tower, their calls noisy and insistent.

It was getting on for six o-clock and the copper fire had been stoked up ready for our baths when I saw the widow next door sitting on a chair in her doorway.

She was busily peeling potatoes (tomorrow's dinner for her brood of ten), taking the skins off with large strokes from a sharp knife, and throwing what was left into a bucket by her side. A sack of cabbage had been propped against the wall, to be dealt with later, she hoped, by some of her friends.

"Can I come and help you?" I called, she nodded and held out a knife. I went over with my stool, picked up a potato and began to peel.

The widow started to sing, and I joined in, feet tapping and hands working as hard as we could. A small fat woman joined us, then another, all sat having a gossip as they dealt with the vegetables.

"You'd best go and see our Tilly," the widow-woman suggested, as the conversation now wasn't intended for my ears, so leaving the knife and half-peeled spud, I went inside her house to find my friend.

She was sitting at a table piled with clothes to mend, reels of cotton and darning wool mixed with tape and elastic in a gaily-covered sewing basket. I found a needle and thread and started to re-make a vest, for a giant it seemed, judging by the size.

Knives chopped or peeled as the women chattered like magpies, the widow louder than any, she was telling them about Lloyd George and the new pension, and you could tell he was really in her good books for doing that.

Someone mentioned he was a Welshman, she mistook the information as a slur on his character, "Yer can say what yer bloomin' likes Missus" her voice thunderous, "but I likes 'im and knows he's a good man."

"I'm sick of all this mending," Tilly said, holding up the pianist's pants, the seat almost non-existent.

"Put a patch on it," shouted the widow stopping her flow of talk to her friends and stomping in.

The girl sighed, picked up a piece of flannel and started to pin it on. She had a queer smile on her face as she mended, and when it was finished, held the garment for me to see, putting a hand over her mouth to stop the laughter.

Round the edges of the patch she'd placed a row of French knots, small hillocks of embroidered cotton that could scrape the hide off a buffalo, then with sniggers and giggles we got up and went into the shed to see if the bath water was hot enough, the night air still filled with the women's voices.

THIS WAS OUR VILLAGE

Chapter Six

SPRING ACTIVITIES

"Hey Gal!" somebody called out in a hoarse whisper, as I stood feeding our pet rabbit Sandy one bitterly cold spring morning.

The hutch had been fastened on to the side of the old stable, tumbledown and with a leaking roof, that together with a tithe barn ran the length of our house, the overhanging thatch giving us a long dry passage to store things.

"Hey, Gal!" the voice was louder now, and almost at my elbow, and through the broken slats, a man's head appeared, thin, white-faced, with a ragged drooping moustache. "Give this to your mother," he went on, head disappearing and an arm thrust out in its place, holding a swede. "Thank 'er for comin' to see to my Missus, and tell 'er she's a lot better this mornin'."

For a second he stood there, tightening the muffler around his neck, and shivered as a blast of cold air poured across through the open door from the yard, then he moved away, and I in turn stood and watched him in the dim light fill the manger full of hay.

Oats were brought in next from a sack standing by a shed, whilst the horses stood, tethered and impatient. Steam rose from their bodies, clouding the oil lamp hanging from the rafters, damp, strong smells drifting upwards caught my nose and throat, making me sneeze and cough in turn.

"Dun't hinder I, Dolly," the man spoke

softly and patiently, as he struggled in the small space to get the mare closer to her food, then Dobbin was shuffled round, and, at last, both stood in the right direction.

Soon, sounds of munching from the animals, and puffing and whistling from the carter, as he groomed and braided, were the only noises to be heard.

As daylight took over from the oil lamp, both horses were ready to start work, the stable given a quick clean up and the animals led to the waggon in the yard.

The man after harnessing them, took the lamp off its hook and blew out the flame, muttering about the "'indrances some blokes got," as he chased out a few stray chickens which had come in for the corn, then closed the bottom half of the door and saw my face looking through the hole.

"Dun't put thee washin' out today Gal,"

he shouted, "we'em 'sheenin' in the barn later on." Then pulling the top half of the stable door too with a bang, he was gone.

I took the swede, and the message, to Ma, wondering if she'd accept it, for only yesterday to give her a treat, my sister and I had helped ourselves to one from the field and brought it home; she didn't even say "thank you," called us "a couple of thieves," made us take it back and stood waiting while we replanted it.

Our eyes met for a half second, she hesitated, then shrugged her shoulders, "Well we can't hurt his feelings," she told me slowly, putting the swede beside the pile of potatoes ready to be peeled.

I was puzzled at that remark, for she hadn't minded hurting mine, yesterday.

It was just after eight o-clock when my friend and I, with her grandfather and several other men, stood waiting in the rickyard behind our house for the threshing machine to arrive.

The old man, wrinkled and horribly bent, started to argue about the waste of money, spent on this "new fangled 'sheen."

"I ought to know, I used the flail in this very barn" we heard, "and the corn was much cleaner, I be sure of that."

"Stop gettin' so windy Dad," replied one of the youths, "and 'elp I to open they barn doors."

"Look, I be go'n to speak out if I wants to" the old man was getting wild, "and I'll punch thy nose if I 'ave any more 'on't."

"Shut thee row Gramp," shouted his grandson over the noise of the traction engine that was just coming in through the gate.

Boys came from behind ricks, and women rushed to take washing off the line, declaring "some folks 'en't got no respect for others," pushed their baskets and children back into their kitchens, shouted some more rude things to the men, and scampered off indoors.

Everyone else stood and admired the large pot-bellied engine and tall chimney, belching out smoke, as slowly and majestically it entered the yard and rolled up to the barn.

Wheels were turned and levers pulled by a man with his cap on back to front, who shouted with a voice of authority to anyone listening, to "Get back now and give I room."

He certainly needed it for fixed by a tow-bar on the back was a long, red, over-sized coffin on wheels.

"Thresher," said the old boy, with contempt, spitting on to the ground and rubbing it in with his boot.

He was taken no notice of, as men surged forward to get it ready, fixing a long flat leather belt from the traction engine to the thresher wheel, and hanging sacks on the receiving end.

The chaff box was opened with a flourish and two men with pitchforks climbed on the straw stacked almost to the roof on one side of the barn, and I with my friend clambered high on to the other pile to watch the fun.

"Cor, bain't we 'igh," said Liz, reaching the top and peeping under the eaves. "Look... they be martins nest," she declared, "ere, lets give 'em a poke wi' that stick."

As I handed it over there was a movement in a far corner of the darkened barn, and umpteen pairs of eyes like little torches dodged about the place.

"Mice" Liz said simply, giving the straw around a whack or two, they disappeared, and we settled down as the men got to work with their pitchforks.

Down came the sheaves of corn into the

mouth of the thresher, dust rose and smoke billowed in, as the wind tore through the open doors, voices were blurred with the noise of the threshing machine and chaff spilled out in every direction.

Soon the corn-filled sacks were replaced with empties, the tops tied with string, then taken to the open doorway and stacked on to the waggon, then Dolly and Dobbin pulled the heavy load, with my friend the carter holding the reins.

As they disappeared from the rickyard the driver turned off the engine, and sent his son, who'd been stoking up the boiler, to the farmhouse for a jug of tea.

Men stamped their feet and waved their arms in an effort to keep warm, letting out a cheer as the boy staggered in with the steaming hot brew. Mugs were quickly filled, mouths wiped with the backs of grimy hands, and loud slurps, coughs and belches reached our ears.

The sun came out for the first time that day, and the men were reluctant to go back to work, so Liz and I decided to leave them and make our get away through a hole in the barn.

"Varmint!" bawled the wrinkled old man as he spotted her. "Come down yer or I'll gi'e thee a thunderin' good 'idin."

"Alright Gramp." The girl slid down off the straw and was given a jolly good wigging, for climbing.

I waited for her by the barn door as she came out minus her stick, and looking very crestfallen. "The old devil wun't let I go back," she said slowly, "not even at the end for the rat killin'."

I was jolly glad, though I didn't say so, as we sauntered up the lane to her home.

"Is that you, Lizzie?" called out a plaintive

voice from inside the house, as we reached the front door, held slightly open by a chain.

"I've been waiting since twelve o-clock for you to return, where on earth have you been?"

"With Gramp and the 'sheenin" the girl replied flatly, unhooking the chain.

I was invited in and for the first time saw the home my friend lived in, small and dark, the only light coming through a tiny un-curtained window, and the flicker from the grate stacked with ashes till it wouldn't hold any more, spilling out on to the dirt floor. The furniture, a square un-scrubbed table and a chair that the woman was sitting on.

She was a gaunt, once good-looking young woman, now with unkempt hair held on top with a single hairpin; her black blouse, unbuttoned halfway down, showed an unnaturally white breast, as she sat feeding a sickly young baby. The air smelt of damp clothes, chimney smoke, and rabbit stew, the latter in a tin bowl boiling on top of the stove.

"Take that to Uncle Jakey," said the mother, pointing to the bowl and a cloth holding some bread. "Don't let him keep you Lizzie, I want you back before its dark."

She noticed me glancing at the shepherds crook in the corner, and told me to go and have a look at it. "That belonged to my great grandfather," she said quietly, with pride in her voice. "We've been shepherds here for a very long time, Jakey's the last of them now." She would have said more but Liz called me, and I was glad to get outside.

Though the sun gave us his company the air was as keen as a knife, and as we walked or sometimes ran the girl explained what the errand was all about.

The shepherd was "Up there lambin'," I

heard, "Mam likes 'im to 'ave 'is 'ot dinner everyday 'cos he might be away for a few weeks," she went on, "and it w'ud be cruel if 'e didn't 'ave some 'ot victuals to look forrard to."

Soon the bleating of lambs and sheep told us we were close to the right field, then we saw the old building and a shepherd's hut.

Liz raced ahead of me and I followed over a muddy track, reaching a stretch of field that had been hurdled off for lambing. On one side a small flock of sheep wandered aimlessly eating; in a smaller pen surrounded by straw, mothers and babies.

The girl called out, and held up the dinner basin to a man working in the far pen, he waved back and carried on with his flock, whilst we found the hut on wheels and climbed aboard.

How cozy it was inside, with a small stove

and a palliasse of straw. We sat down on the floor, took our boots off and warmed our feet until Uncle Jakey made his appearance.

He was dressed in a thick rough smock and a billycock hat that must have belonged to his father, sturdy trousers and gaiters and mud-plastered boots.

A newly born lamb was held firmly under one arm, it was wrapped in an old coat and laid gently by the stove to recover.

"Will it be alright?" I asked the man, never having seen such a young animal before.

"You wait till 'is belly's filled," he answered with a laugh, "he'll be skippin' in no time at all."

All that afternoon we stayed, giving the lamb drinks and doing odd jobs around the fold. I saw sheep die and lambs born, feeling sad and happy in turn.

"Can't allus keep them all," replied the

shepherd to my question, "that en't nature's way of doin' things at all."

"Do you miss them, when they die or go to market?" I looked at him closely.

"Only for a little while," he replied.

The sky was now dark blue, pin-cushioned with golden stars, as I turned and walked at the backs of the houses, remembering the rabbit had to be fed.

He sat there, facing me boldly and unmoving.

"Sandy," I whispered softly, pushing some cabbage leaves through the wire netting, "today I've found out many things but I can't tell you yet, 'cos they're secret Liz says, and she knows everything."

THIS WAS OUR VILLAGE

Chapter Seven

RELATIVES

"My grandmother's coming today," I told Gertie, pleased that at last I'd be able to show off a relative for a change.

"Stayin' with yer for good?" she asked casually, her thin hands pushing the woollen jumper, all unravelled at the bottom, into her tight-fitting skirt.

"If she is," her voice held a warning note, "you'll find her a bloody nuisance."

"See this?" my friend went on, opening the lid of a wicker basket filled to the brim with clean washing. "Our Mam does that

for Gran every week; she goes and fetches it,
I takes it back, and sees Gran remembers to
'ave 'er weekly wash-down and change. Two
miles, winter and summer I goes, she's nothin'
else but a bloomin' old pest."

Gertie hoisted herself on to the wall and
pulled the basket up beside her, pushed her
feelings into the background, and began to
sing, whilst I went indoors to get ready.

She was a tall noisy girl, all black
stockings and heavily studded boots, "common"
my mother called her, and rarely asked her in
when she came to our house, but today even
Ma agreed that her voice was lovely and
ought to be trained, "and if something could be
done about her manners," Ma pursed her lips,
"you never knew, she might, one day become
a lady."

As if to contradict what had been said,
the girl jumped down off the wall and broke

into a jiggy dance, wriggling her hips and shouting at the top of her voice the latest song, 'Bye Bye Blackbird'.

Ma shuddered and turned away from the window, and handed me a pair of Dad's Sunday shoes to be dropped in at the cobblers. He, like my friend's Gran, lived across the fields in the next village.

We sauntered off on our errands with a small bag of buns to share between us, passing the rookery alive with birds, some staking a claim to the old nests, others, small swaying back blobs, just waiting an opportunity. Twigs and dirt fell in all directions as we stood underneath, looking up.

"Ever 'ad rook pie?" Gert asked, a smile of real pleasure coming over her face at the memory, "Our Mam put seventeen of they in the last one she made, with a pastry top sprinkled wi' parsley."

I couldn't bear to think of all those birds held tightly under the pie-crust, and turned my attention to the man in the next field, who, with three horses, was hand ploughing.

Up and down he walked in long straight lines, leaving the chalky white stripes to the dipping, screaming gulls following behind him.

"Uncle Ted," my friend bawled out as she spotted another of her umpteen relations working on his own plot. He turned, saw who it was, and started to walk over to us, unfastening a strap across his chest which held what I thought was a violin, though why he should be wanting to play on a muddy bit of ground, and so low down on his body, I couldn't imagine.

"'Tain't no violin," the girl said, laughing, "'tis a seed planter. En't yer seen one afore?"

"Hey, Ted," she called out in great voice though he was close at hand, "come over yer and show 'er 'ow you duz it."

I saw a square-ish wooden box, half filled with seed, and a small wheel attached to the bottom.

"Now watch I sow," said the lad. Fastening the contraption on to his person, he fixed a wood and thong bow on to the small wheel, then with his right hand drew it right and left across his body.

Instantly the seed fell out, spraying in alternate directions.

"Twelve feet each side it spreads," he boasted, walking slowly in front of us and steadily bowing.

"Old farmer bought that for our Dad," I was told by Gert as we made our way slowly to the cress beds. "Said 'twould be quicker than old kidney bean basket and spreadin' seed wi'

two hands, but our Dad wouldn't 'ave nothin'
to do wi' it."

We crossed the stile by the stream, shallow
and weedy, several men were there standing at
the side trying to clean it out, others tidying
the hedges and lopping branches off trees;
everywhere there seemed to be activity.

A couple of them moved away from the
group, dropped their billhooks and started to
make a bonfire. Dead wood, branches, hedge
cuttings and old straw were gathered into a
huge mound, paraffin poured on liberally
from a tin can and set alight.

Tongues of flame, like long red demons,
leapt higher than the pile, followed by blue
smoke, cracking and spitting sounds, as the
whole host of rubbish caught fire.

We pressed forward to enjoy the warmth
and got turned back by an angry workman,
cupping his hands he yelled out, "Missus?"

From the garden behind us a woman's head and shoulders appeared above the hedge, there were children's voices and piglets squealing.

"Thought I telled yer to keep they kids away from 'ere" he shouted to her, swinging his rake with a savage movement.

There was a clanking sound as a bucket was stood on the ground, and a sweet sickly smell of warm pigswill met our nostrils. We turned and met a pair of eyes almost closed with rage, and a voice that equally matched them.

"They kids bain't mine," she hissed, "never seed 'am afore. Must be 'foreigners' thats cum from t'other village."

While they argued we crept passed the woman's house, using the shelter of the hedge for our get away.

"Bet she's a witch," Gert whispered, as we

sped on, "and did you notice how she hissed at that man?"

"I'm sure there was a besom by the backdoor" I replied.

At the end of the narrow lane close to the farm that had POST OFFICE written over the doorway stood two cottages, thatched roofed, with black beams clearly outlined on the cream walls.

"'Ere we are then'', my friend braced her shoulders and looking determined, kicked open the garden gate nearest to us, and marched up the pathway.

"Gran!" she bawled, giving the knocker such a mighty thump that the rusty horseshoe fairly danced on its one screw.

"Gran!" she shouted again, turning the handle on the door and poking her head in gingerly to see if all was well. "I've brought thee washin' and me friend along to see thee."

Out from another room came an old lady,
looking like an oversized dressed up cottage
loaf, her head covered with a bonnet, an old
flowered gray shawl round her shoulders held
by a silver brooch with 'Mother' inscribed on it.

She was as deaf as a post, so everything
we wanted her to know came at the tops of our
voices or by hand signs.

"Hullo Phyllis" she greeted me, patting
my hair, and I thought she had mistaken me
for one of her dead daughters.

"Dun't waste time wi' 'er." said Gert, as
I started to explain things to Gran. "Let's get
firewood in and a bit of grub ready, or I can see
we'll be 'ere till bloody Sunday."

Logs were chopped down into burnable
sizes and stacked where they could be reached
in the scullery, the fire made up and the
kettle put on, a list of groceries written down
and a rice pudding popped into the oven.

Later with a cup of tea and some home-
made gingerbread, Gran's ear trumpet found and
put into position, we all sat clustered round
the fire and heard what had been going on.

"Postman had left," Gran said, "you
know, the one that lived in the mud hut
halfway up village. Uncle Jakey's found
hisself a housekeeper, a young girl straight
from orphanage, fourteen that's all she is,"
went on Gran, "and he works her night and
day, like a nigger."

The rest of the news was cut short by my
friend suddenly noticing the time.

"Where's thee bag then?" she interrupted,
getting up and collecting the grocery list off
the table, "Can't carry all thee wants in me
arms now, can I?" the bantering tone of her
voice made us all laugh.

With a speed that surprised me the old
girl darted into the scullery, returning with

a long canvas bag in one hand and a Toby jug in the other.

"Will you get us a pint of stout?" she asked, pushing the jug into Gert's hand, then noticing the protest forming on the girl's lips, "You've got to pass the place haven't you?" she wheedled.

The money for the shopping was found a few minutes later, after much searching among'st her many petticoats, then weary with her effort, she sat down and closed her eyes, instantly forgetting us.

It was pub opening time when the shopping was finished, and Gert led the way to the 'Jug and Bottle' department (a small passage, white-washed, about four feet wide which led to a highly polished bar counter at the other end).

Behind it stood a thick set man with a polished head, busily filling bottles and jugs by pulling down a white-topped lever in front of him, froth rose and poured down the sides as he set them on the counter in front of the boy or girl heading the queue.

"Pint of twos please" or "half of fours" (twopence or fourpence a pint) I heard, as warm tobacco smoke and a beery smell enveloped me. Why did Ma say these places were "hotbeds of sin and misery" and watched she never went inside one of them? All I could hear was laughter, swear words and scuffing feet, and now and again the sound of a mouth organ being played.

The Toby jug was filled and carried back carefully by me down the village street, as my friend was reluctant to have anything to do with it.

"Filthy stuff," she said bitterly, "I tries to keep 'er off but like our Mam, she can't seem to live wi'out it." For a second or two the girl looked very upset, then her mood changed to its usual defiance.

It was close on one o-clock before the groceries had been checked and put into the pantry, a cloth placed halfway over the kitchen table, the Toby jug, glass and a spoon put close to Gran's elbow.

"Let's see thee eat fust." Gert slapped the dish of rice in front of the old girl, and poured a generous helping of cold milk over to cool it.

The remark was ignored by the old woman, as a trembling hand filled the glass with stout. It was raised and emptied with hardly a pause, and followed by loud "ah"s of pleasure, as she filled it up to the brim again.

"Come on Gran, get that puddin' down, I wants to see it finished 'fore I goes home." The girl's voice rose with exasperation, as she moved from the table and put her coat on.

The clock had ticked a good ten minutes before the old girl obliged, and the last orders were shouted from the doorway by her granddaughter.

"Dun't forget to 'ave thee good wash tonight, and change they clothes ready for Mam when she comes, Monday mornin."

My friend and I parted at the cobbler's house, for Gert was late as it was for her dinner, and her mother, unlike mine, made no allowances for running errands, so if she was quick in reaching home she might get half a dinner, if too late there wouldn't be any.

A large green tin shed stood at the bottom of the cobblers garden, with a faded name plate on a piece of card in the window. A long bony mongrel lying full length across the mat got up, slowly stretched, yawned and then sat scratching itself.

Once inside it didn't look like a shed at all, with the floor covered with coconut matting from door to counter, and a round black stove belching out heat and smoke in the corner, making the eyes water till you got used to it.

The snob (shoe mender), a fattish man with a wooden leg, and wearing a leather apron and his war medals, sat with a boot on an iron foot between his knees, a squashy finger and thumb going regularly to his mouth lifting a brad out one at a time and knocking them into the edge of the boot with his hammer.

For a full hour I sat on a stool and waited, whilst a couple of toecaps were shaped and fixed on to Dad's shoes, the edges blacked round with something on a thin stick, polished and a new pair of laces added.

The cobbler then wrapped both in a brown paper parcel and said "You tell your Dad I'll let 'im know what the damage is when next I see 'im."

I thanked him and was gone, taking long strides and sometimes running in my eagerness to get home and see our visitor.

The bonfire by the hedge was out, and not a sign of the old woman or her children; the stream large and singing now, with all the weeds and dead cress gone.

Rooks still called and squabbled amongst themselves. Gulls, spread like pepper and salt, ate their way steadily over the new-tilled soil.

It was just starting to rain when I arrived back home, washed my face and decided to put on a clean dress, when a car drove up and Ma got out looking rather flustered, then she helped someone out calling her "Grandma."

What a tiny woman our relation was, I thought she looked just like Queen Victoria's photo, all black lace, ribbons and embroidered petticoat, ringed fingers, bracelets, and a long gold chain with a pair of spectacles on the end of it.

"En't she posh," Gert exclaimed the next day, coming early for school to have a jolly good look at her, and my heart filled with pride when she told all her friends "'Er Gran's like old Squire's widder only much nicer."

But my grandmother let me down a few nights later, when I returned home with a spiteful girl I was trying to impress.

There sat Dad with his mother, by the light of an oil lamp, eating jellied pig's trotters with slices of brown bread, and right beside them, where the girl could clearly see, was a bottle of beer, a smaller one labelled GIN, and a jug holding water to top up her glass.

THIS WAS OUR VILLAGE

Chapter Eight

EASTER

It was Good Friday, and a holiday, but at seven o-clock in the morning the village was already astir.

The carters had gone to work just after three, whilst it was still dark with a cutting wind blowing, hobnailed boots rattling on the stony lane close to my bedroom window.

Horses were being watered and fed, stables cleaned and hay-racks refilled. The voices of the men talking to each other as they moved around, carried on the cold morning air.

Soon they'd return for breakfast, and

when that was over, the great 'planting session' in gardens and allotments would start, filling most of the daylight hours that remained.

Everyone put their potatoes in on Good Friday, it was the village tradition, and outside each house stood a wheelbarrow or handcart, old pram or pushchair, loaded with seed potatoes or manure.

Children dressed in cut-me-downs and worn out boots brought rakes and hoes from the sheds, using them as 'hobby horses' as they rushed up and down the garden path.

"Stop messin' about" they were told, as tools snatched from their grasp were quickly tied on carriers, and when all was ready, anyone old enough to be useful left with the men and their loads a short time later.

We were up early enough, and as eager as the rest to be away, but father felt different;

he was in no hurry to prepare for the garden spree. To avoid my mother's exasperated remarks he fetched water from the well, pumped up the tyres on his bike, moved the oil lamp from the front bracket and filled it, polished its mirror-like glass window for the umpteenth time and fixed it back on. Ma fretted for him to go, taking us with him so that she could get on with some work, but he wouldn't be pushed.

At last, when every barrow and cart had gone, those who had gardens or ground close to home hard at it, we made our move.

Pa brought the brand new rake and hoe from the coal shed and fixed it with string to the crossbar of the bike, tested the new dibber for quality, wiped it and pushed it in his belt, humped a sack of spuds on to the saddle, and at last, we were ready to depart.

Up the long street the three of us walked

solemnly, my sister and I either side holding the load. Father, like a king, took his place at the front, both hands gripping the handlebars to prevent disaster.

We arrived at the allotment about half an hour later, Pa stopping just before reaching the first plot, and pretending to check the sack, gave out his request, in a voice that was barely a whisper.

"You keep your eyes on old Benny's planting of potatoes, how wide apart and deep," he went on, "and I'll see how he manages his onion sowing, whilst I stand there giving him a chat up."

Somewhat surprised at his suggestion, having in the past been told not to be nosey, but knowing that you can never account for parents, we did as we were asked and had a good look.

Old Benny was down to his last row of

spuds, as father started up a long conversation, whilst the man measured and dibbed, put the firm seed shoot uppermost in the ground as we stood there, gaining experience.

Onions were next, for Benny never varied the planting of his allotment. A well worn hoe was used to draw a fine line in the soil about an inch deep, seed sprinkled then soil lightly covered over and firmed down with the old man's heavy boot.

Having learned the lessons unwittingly given by our friend, the three of us moved on, passing several plots and gardeners calling to one another about the state of the ground, weather and chances of getting a decent crop, questions and answers bandied too and fro till we reached our barren patch.

The top half of our plot looked like a wilderness, liberally sown with bottles, broken glass and bits of an old shed, then came a nice sized piece of newly weeded ground and at the bottom a row of rusty buckets with sprouting rhubarb.

Dad rested the bike carefully against the hedge, looked at the scene and sighed mightily, the sack was brought over and tools laid out on the ground; then a general shedding of coats, which were tied on to the handlebars, bootlaces tightened, and we were ready to begin.

A few minutes of Pa's gardening convinced me he was new to the job, each hole had to be measured and dibbed in the 'Benny' manner, and earth scraped over or removed, as we argued amongst ourselves how deep to put them in. Finally, potatoes with eyes pointing heavenwards got pushed in by me, my sister following closely behind covered them with stony soil.

Up one row, down the other we plodded,

sending messages hot-foot to the Almighty for a speedy end to our misery and toil, but they couldn't have reached Him for as the last spud was dropped into its hole, father had another task ready for us.

From his pocket he drew out a packet and split it open, pouring some of the tiny onion seeds into the palm of his hand, commanding us at the same time, to "Hurry up quick and make a thin trench." I made a wobbly line with the hoe and he bent over to sprinkle the seed with finger and thumb. The wind, catching the packet, tossed it high into the air, dispensing with great prodigality the contents over our neighbour's plot.

We pressed on with the sowing, raked the earth in and trod it down with our boots, retrieved the now empty packet and fastened it to the end of the row with a twig.

The first attempt with the allotment

had succeeded despite our ignorance, and it was now time to go home. Tools were cleaned with a sharp stone, wrapped in the empty sack and fixed to the bike, boots removed and cleaned with a stick and some grass, put back on and retied.

Back along the path we walked with an air of great confidence, meeting 'old Benny's stare with our own.

"E'nt you puttin' nothin' else in?" he asked Dad, surprised that we weren't stopping the whole day, his own plot nearly completed and labelled with orderly rows.

"Wish I could," came the airy reply from Pa as he mounted his bike, "but I'm taking the wife out this afternoon."

How my sister and I laughed at the answer the old man got, as we strolled into the shop for some sweets leaving Dad to get a pint at the Squire's Arms, for we knew with certainty that more information from someone would have to be forthcoming, before our carrots and beans could be dealt with.

* * * * * *

Saturday morning greeted us with a clear sky and warm sunshine. We were going primrosing.

So would several other villagers, but not all together; nobody minded the odd swede or turnip gone, or perhaps give a bit of help when needed, but disclosing the whereabouts of anything free, like blackberries or mushrooms, firewood or wild flowers — well, that was an entirely different matter.

So when I saw my friends go quietly past the house, and later on their parents in the same direction, I didn't call out, for I knew we'd meet again in the afternoon, down at the copse two miles away.

Waiting for the rest of our family to

join me, I remembered the very first primrose outing.

It was too far then for my sister and I to walk, so Dad had taken us in turn on his bike. A cushion strapped on to the carrier at the back hadn't softened the bumps from the uneven road. I was taken the first mile, put down on to the narrow pathway and told to keep walking till he returned, then he turned the bike round and cycled back for my sister.

Today we could all manage the four miles across the fields, starting at the right of way through the farmyard.

Skirting the hayricks to avoid the turkeys, who if they caught sight of us would come streaming over gobbling and shaking their wattles, we chose the side where chickens pecked at the side of a dirty pond, weed-cluttered and smelly.

"Don't let us hang about long," cautioned

Dad, as we stopped to look at the ducks, and a sheep dog pulled itself slowly on to its legs and started to move in our direction.

On past the cart sheds and over the turnpike road, to a rutted track, muddy and in places waterlogged.

"Get on to the edge of the field" called out Pa, as the cardboard soles of our boots let in the water almost immediately. I climbed up the small bank and noticed for the first time the flat fields on either side, pale green with spring grass, heard bird song and saw pheasants strutting, the air crystal clear, and the view spreading for miles.

The track ended at two farm cottages with tumbledown outhouses. A flaxen-haired girl leaned on a gate, swinging it gently to and fro, the toe of one boot split, showing part of a pink foot.

"Hallo Annie," I called out (for she came

to our school).

"Dad's making a scarecrow" she told me, pointing to a man in the garden busy wrapping straw round a thin long stick, but I was looking behind him to a string line held between two poles, with a row of dead stoats strung along it.

"They be a warnin' to all they other stoats," she informed me matter-of-factly, as my gaze kept wandering from her to the line beyond.

Pa had finished his conversation with the scarecrow maker and was ready to move on, when he spotted the old cart-horse in the gateway.

"Well I'm blowed," he said, smiling with pleasure at seeing her. "Thought you'd gone for good, Daisy old girl." He whistled softly like he used to, the animal recognised his voice, whinnied, tossed her head and clomped the ground.

Dad hunted in his pockets for the sugar lumps he never seemed to be without, and asked his friend why she'd been "poked down here for heavens sake?"

"'Cos she was due for the slaughter yard," we heard, "but I couldn't let 'er down, not arter all these ye'rs we 'ad together, so I told farmer I'd feed 'er me'self and yer she is." Dad patted and stroked the horse, who responded by nuzzling into his arm.

"Cherio," shouted Annie to me as we stood by the corner and waved our goodbyes, Dad looking very pleased at meeting his old four-legged friend again.

Our path led through an orchard with apple and plum trees, the blossom just showing in soft pink and white buds, then we crossed the stile and a deep drop to the water meadows, full of rushes and golden kingcups.

"Watch the hummocks," Pa called out, nimbly jumping from one soggy tuft to the next, the ground being covered in no time at all and only one pair of feet missing the firm bank by the stream.

Moorhens hearing us raced to the far side of the water, taking their broods with them. The bright eyes of a rat watched the scene from a hole close to our feet, decided it was safe to go and swam in a straight line to the other bank.   Flat on our stomachs we drew our hands through the water, letting frogspawn trickle past our fingers.

Voices could be heard in the distance, the copse must be close now, on the opposite side of the railway line.

Shouting and listening to the echoes, we passed through the low dark tunnel, and on coming out again into the daylight saw the wonderful sight of the primroses.

Like a thick lemon carpet they led from the pathway into the distance, the delicate scent on the breeze filled the warm spring air.

Soon the wicker basket we'd brought was lined with damp moss and the picking began, taking only those just coming out as we'd been instructed to do.

With the basket and two large paper bags nearly filled we turned into the broad path and met up with some of the villagers.

"What took 'ee so long to get yer?" we were asked, "We'm finished and thinkin of goin' 'ome soon," but they waited, putting their baskets on the ground and sitting on an old log watched my father.

He'd found some soft green rushes by the stream, and was now busy weaving them into a shape of a nest, and when he'd finished placed it carefully in a string bag, then brushing the odd bits of rubbish from his trousers stood up ready for the long trek back.

We continued on the wide path, flowers spilling to the ground from the overloaded baskets and bags carried by the grown ups, whilst children of all ages and sizes rushed on gaily through the woods and back to the stream.

What talking and laughter of outings long ago, what singing and fun we all had, till the sun felt it had had enough, and sank down over the distant hill.

After tea that same evening, bowls of primroses were taken to the big church, to be mixed with narcissi and tulips into gorgeous displays for Easter Sunday, and we watched whilst a lady placed our bowl of flowers on a windowsill that was decorated with moss and dark blue hyacinths.

Easter Sunday morning was rather special in our house and started with game of 'hunt the egg' (they were real eggs dyed red and green and hidden in secret places by my mother).

When they'd all been found we went back into the kitchen and had a rare treat, bacon and sausage breakfast with fried bread and tomatoes. Ma hadn't forgotten the cat either; he had the chopped up rind from the bacon in his bread and milk.

After everyone had finished and the table cleared of plates and cutlery, presents were brought in, one painted cardboard box for each child, with a small felt chicken standing on the lid, and inside, packed tightly in tissue paper, a tiny chocolate Easter egg.

It was now time to give Dad and Mum our presents; three bantams eggs, and a pheasant feather that we'd found.

In the midst of the unwrapping and egg tasting Pa disappeared, returning a few moments later with the rush nest that he'd made in the copse; it was filled with blue and white scented violets, and handing them to Ma neither said a word, but I noticed after the flowers had died the nest was wrapped in a piece of silk and locked with her private things, in the big trunk.

THIS WAS OUR VILLAGE

Chapter Nine

MAY DAY

"That bloomin' lot next door sound like a hive of bees" remarked my father, as he came into the kitchen carrying two full buckets of water that he'd drawn from the well before going off to work.

Ma looked out of the window on the activity. "It's May Day" she reminded him. "They're getting their flowers ready for the celebration."

Crash! went the widow's back door once again, as three children rushed across to the shed, reappearing a few seconds later with two longish stout poles and a tin bucket crammed with flowers.

The youngest of the brood, known as 'our babe', staggered behind rolling a ball of binder twine almost as big as herself to the door, slipped, and with one foot in the mud, let out a mighty roar.

A large ham-bone of a hand shot out and grabbed her and a voice from the curtained window threatened, "The next lot as goes outside this room gets a 'idin', and I mean it."

A grey tabby cat wound its sleek body round my legs as I stood outside by the chestnut tree enjoying the morning, tapping its head against my ankles now and again to remind me breakfast was long overdue.

I picked it up and was about to go in when the widow woman opened her door and came out, holding a large pair of scissors.

Her round shiny face looked for all the

world as though she'd used the scrubbing brush on it, and her hair, drawn into a tight bun at the back, showed a pair of very bright pink ears. She was swathed in a flowing chintz overall, well pinched in at the middle.

"Bide quiet and give I time to think." she shouted out from halfway down the path to the crowd of children standing in her doorway, all speaking at once in their efforts to make her hurry.

"E'nt picking they" she murmured to herself, turning away from a clump of peonies, brilliant red blooms inside the low box hedge, "Nor they gillies, them's me favourites," she moved on and stood looking at the next flower bed.

"Mam," the voice whined, "Mam, cans't thee 'urry up, procession starts at eight."

The woman turned as though to reprimand, spotted the shrub my mother had planted against the house, and came slowly up the path to inspect.

It was a china rose, now in full bloom, long delicate sprays, green leaved and studded with fluffy orange-coloured balls, which over the years had never been pruned and spilled over into the widows garden.

For a second she stood there, one thick finger and thumb stroking the scissors blade.

"Wun't be able to open me winder soon, if I dun't 'ave a couple of they off pretty smartish," I heard.

Her eyes looked rather guilty as they met mine, then with a quick snip two of the largest flower-laden stems were in her hand, and she vanished wearing a slow smile of satisfaction.

At eight o'clock, the procession appeared, and halted at the bottom of our lane.

Two older girls headed the procession of children, with starched white pinafores worn over long dresses, on their hair a circlet of lilys-of-the-valley. Each carried a tall pole, held by both hands high in front of them, the pole decorated with primroses, forget-me-nots, wallflowers, and garden bluebells, and crowned with lilies and white lilac.

Boys followed holding smaller poles with cowslips, pansies and large coloured daises wound around it, and topped with tulips. More children from a house nearby swelled the party to a long thin stream; we took our places dressed in white lace, and holding in our hands ribboned posies.

Just at the last minute, when everyone seemed ready, came the widow's offspring, each with their tall poles crowned with the china roses.

The long procession started to move, watched by mothers with babies in arms, and toddlers clinging to their long cotton skirts.

Old people stood in doorways or leaned over

windowsills, talking of the "old days and how they used to exchange ribbons."

Holding our flowers aloft and walking slowly, we chanted

"Remember today is the first of May,
And we have come a-garlanding."

This was repeated over and over again, with breaks to stop at a large house to sing a spring song, till the main streets of the village had all been trodden and the school bell reminded us that lessons would soon begin.

I returned home and placed my posy in a vase, the joy of garlanding on a spring morning was over for another year.

＊＊＊＊＊

School finished at twelve o'clock, but Mayday wasn't quite finished with, for our class had been asked to give a dancing display in the afternoon, at Parson's request, at the

Vicarage.

On the well-clipped lawn stood a maypole, red and blue braids swinging gently in the warm breeze, and seated around it, on forms and garden chairs, were Mums and Dads, babies, and some of the gentry. Boys rushed about the green, rolling over and over in the soft turf.

"Come back yer," shouted a young woman, dragging one of hers reluctantly back to his seat, "We'll lose our place if yer dun't behave, and I wants to see our Jimmy do the dancin'."

'Jimmy' was with the rest of us, waiting for the Vicar's wife to hand out our costumes.

"I be off if she dun't turn up soon," Jimmy said sullenly. His feet drummed on the glass panel of the French window, "Didn't want to do it in the fust place."

He was interrupted by his friend, who'd

been giving the room beyond his undivided attention,

"Coo, look at all they chairs and tables," his voice filled with admiration, "and that gert clock wi' a name written round the face." He pressed his face closer to the glass to try and read what it said.

At that moment the Vicar's wife chose to spoil his view; five feet of mauve silk, feather boa, and hat covered with parma violets. Holding her long skirt with one delicate gloved hand, she unclipped the door and with a look of utter disgust at our manners asked us to follow her in.

We crossed the room that smelt as though it rarely had an airing, through the hallway and up the broad, heavily carpeted stairs.

"Better'n Squire's house" was Jim's verdict after taking a good look round, as he waited to be fitted with a green cotton shirt, and paper Robin Hood hat decorated with a single chicken feather.

Our dresses too were green, floor length and with low-necked bodices, pulled in tight with white lacing, and over them a yellow apron and for our hair a white frilled mobcap. Soon we were dressed and ready for the inspection.

The Vicar's wife looked us up and down very carefully, and clearly didn't like at all what she saw. We younger girls were dismissed and told to put our plimsoles on in the hall, ready for dancing. After a few minutes four older girls appeared on the stairs, wearing little capes of net curtaining round their shoulders and tied in a discreet bow across their bosoms.

Up the broad steps and on to the green we ran, hand in hand with a boy as our partner, the crowd cheered and clapped as each child took their place around the maypole and held a braid.

The fiddler struck a chord, we bowed and started to dance in time to the tune, weaving red braid over blue till a fine check appeared down the pole. The music stopped, we turned and bowed to each other again, dancing in the opposite direction till the check pattern disappeared and the braids ran free in our hands.

There was "Well done," and from Jim's Mum, "Jim, yer did it beautiful."

The ribbons were left hanging and the dancing quickly forgotten as with a rattle of tambourines and singing at the tops of their voices, six 'gypsies' appeared from the kitchen garden. Skins browned with burnt cork, heads firmly tied with cotton headscarves, earrings swinging, skirts swirling like giant sticks of peppermint rock as with bare feet they made their way in our direction. Round the forms and chairs they danced, shaking their tambourines, till babies cried on mothers laps at the din. Then with a last wild leap and a bang they were gone, and a violin started to play 'Greensleeves' or so the ladies told us.

Buns and tea, sandwiches and biscuits followed, which Parson had announced as "an interlude," and posh ladies walked around dressed as serving maids, holding baskets over their arms filled with bags of sweets, oranges, and monkey nuts.

At last all the eating was finished, the chairs and forms moved to another part of the garden, then everyone got into their dancing positions and, with a "one, two" from the leader and the fiddler in full play, started the country dancing.

Right foot, left foot, turn around, new steps mixed with old ones, then it was time to stop, and we all stood around, whilst Vicar thanked us for coming.

"Not at all" boomed the voice of an ex-
singer, who'd just come to live in the village
and felt he should be spokesman for all of us,
"We're indebted to you Sir," he went on.

"Well both of thee make thee minds up
so I can clap and go 'ome," muttered a woman
who looked tired, and had a whimpering baby
beside me.

They apparently did for the clapping
began, and people started drifting down the
stone steps, homeward.

We were the last to leave, taking our caps
and dresses off, folding them away in the old
chest for another time, then "goodnight" to the
parrot half asleep on his perch in the hall, as
the maid locked the big gates behind us.

Dad heard all the news as we walked
up the lane together, and saw the decorated
poles in the windows of the widow's house, and

he saw our posies, still in the china jug, and
listened whilst we sang the chant he'd missed
in the morning;

> "Remember today is the first of May,
> And we have come a-garlanding."

THIS WAS OUR VILLAGE

Chapter Ten

FEAST WEEK

The first day of summer in our village was celebrated on Whit Sunday, when regardless of the weather we'd cast off winter woollies and don our new clothes. For me it meant a new dress, white and with tiny sprigs of flowers round the sleeves and hem, a cream straw hat held under the chin with thin round elastic, short white socks and new sandals.

Whit Sunday was a magical day for another reason; it was the beginning of FEAST WEEK, which began at six o-clock in the evening when the field by the old pub would be filled with the makings of a fair. There'd be other things, like a 'Cheap Jack' stall or bowling for a pig, but tonight we were all standing in the main street, waiting for the horse-drawn caravans to arrive.

Women passed in stiff black hats with veils, there were silk ones covered with cotton roses. Boys in long black stockings and boots cleaned with soot from the chimney, men wearing new caps that had plaited straw 'favours' fixed to the peak at the front – and there was my father in his boater with a cord hanging from it and on the end a clip that held it firmly to the collar of his coat.

It seemed ages before someone (who'd been posted at the corner) shouted out "its here," and we all pushed and shoved to get the first glance of the caravans and carts, the gypsies and their children, donkeys and a horde of dogs that always seemed to follow them.

Once in the field, they started to unload, and we children stood behind the wire fence watching, whilst some of the parents returned home and others stopped at the pub to celebrate the beginning of a week's fun.

Thin, rough looking men unhitched the horses and led them to the bottom of the meadow, tethering them by long ropes amongst the buttercups and grass, then returned and jumped up on to the heavily laden trailers and began to pull off the swing boats and rods.

Horses neighed and dogs barked, men swore and their women-folk shouted, as parts of stalls, coconut shies, boxes and wrapped up tent tops were hauled from the carts and heaped everywhere. Only the traction engine, which had drawn the makings of a roundabout, stood aloof, puffing black smoke into the night air.

"We ought to be getting home," shouted my sister from her perch on a beer crate, but we both hung on waiting for the rock to be made and just when we'd given up hope and decided to go, a caravan door opened and a stout woman in a black dress and large gold earrings came down the steps.

She was carrying a tray with two long roly-poly-looking things on it, one cream-coloured, the other a chocolate brown, and setting it down chose the cream one and folded it round a metal upright that was holding up the fence.

Two hands fixed the loose ends and like a skein of wool it was pulled out and tossed back over the upright and pulled down, again and again the woman tossed and pulled till the skein looked eventually like silk.

Then the brown one was treated in the very same manner and when smooth, both

were plaited together. The woman wiped her
hands on her apron, picked up a small pair of
shears, cut the rock into sizeable pieces and
laid them in rows on the tray, they were then
taken back into the caravan to dry.

We ran all the way home, for it was now
getting late, thoroughly satisfied with what
we'd seen and knowing that if we could get
enough pennies there'd be fun for the rest of
the week.

On Monday evening our first visit was
to the 'Cheap Jack', who had set up a stall
in the yard of one of the pubs. It was filled to
overflowing with cups, saucers and plates,
basins, jugs, cake bowls and stone jars. There
was a complete toilet set with two oval
dishes, and a large water jug standing in a
washbasin. All had beautiful mauve pansies
painted on the outside, and the two chamber
pots had matching designs inside and out.

The 'Cheap Jack', a short fat confident man dressed in a dirty mac', and bowler hat perched at an angle on the back of his head, stood on an old orange box, his feet in patent leather boots doing a kind of tap dance, as he swung this way and that to his customers.

"It's a free night tonight," he was shouting, "see, I'm starving meself to death to help you." The diamond shone in the ring on his finger as he held up two cups and a plate. "I'll take twopence for this lot." His eyes looked down at mine, "What about these for your mother, girlie?"

"I've only a penny" I told him and fled.

The following night my sister and I sat having our tea and we hadn't a halfpenny between us. Ma was sick in bed with "one of her turns," which even the bottles of white stuff she kept drinking, didn't seem to help.

Dad was in no mood to be generous either,

for he was getting ready to fetch the Doctor,
four miles away, and tell Ma's friend "would
she please come along."

"And don't forget the tot of whisky for her
present," Ma called from the bedroom.

We gave him a pleading look, as
grumbling, he passed us, for the Doctor at the
moment was his pet hate, after the last visit
when Pa had his body-belt confiscated, and
told to "have cold baths every morning, man,
and do without your vest now it's springtime."

Having no luck we toyed for a long time
with the idea of asking Ma, changed our minds
and argued between ourselves who should do
the washing up.

Sometime later Ma's friend and Dad
came in, "Thought you'd both be at the fair"
he muttered.

"We haven't any money" both of us
blubbered. He went over to the mantelpiece

and opened a box, gave us three pennies each, without a word.

Amazed at his behaviour we scuttled off before he could change his mind, running up the steep hill by the cemetery, and heard the sounds of the organ coming over the houses, drawing us to the fair like a magnet.

Never had a roundabout looked so beautiful as this one, with its gaily coloured lights and striped awning overhead, and as it swung round we spelled out the owners name, in gold lettering, each letter divided with a red painted rose.

Twisted brass rods seemed to go right through the carved wooden horses and cockerels, their legs and eyes showing they were ready to be off.

I climbed on to the small horse that had a pale yellow tossed mane, and had 'Beauty' written in green on her shoulder, and I couldn't help stroking her smooth silky neck as I waited for the ride to begin.

In front of the organ, moving a fan jerkily over her face, a blue figurine in a crinoline gown, and at her side, busily beating a small drum, a tiny soldier in military hat and breeches.

A man with a brass bell gave it a couple of clouts with a short stick, the steam engine ceased its hissing and we started to move. I pressed my knees into 'Beauty's side; we rose and fell in great galloping leaps.

Lights flashed by, people became one long blur. I heard parts of 'Sheikh of Araby' as we circled, then the brakes went on hard, and we came back to earth with a shudder.

Gone was the magic of flying, I got off the horse, my legs feeling like paper, and staggered from the platform.

The tune changed to 'Clementine'. I wandered over to a fat man, who in shirt sleeves was trying to lift some weights, then on to the coconut shies and youths who were accusing the fairman of "sticking they nuts in with glue, they were sure," as not one coconut moved for all their tries.

Flares had been lit and hung one to each stall, boys chased in and out of the crowds with water squirters, there was a fish and chip smell mixed with paraffin and hot engine oil, and now and again whiffs of beer and cheap tobacco.

A man was trying to shoot a ping pong ball floating in the air on a jet of water, missed, and I heard the ring as shot met the metal sheet protecting the canvas. Someone shouted "HELP," people dashed to the scene and found a woman kneeling on the ground trying to find her false teeth, which had fallen out as she laughed with fright whilst flying skywards in a swing boat.

Darkness and the cold night air told us it was getting late. I spent my last halfpenny on the rock I'd seen made, then found my sister and we both sped homewards, taking the short cut across our neighbour's garden.

Father was sitting by the fire smoking his pipe. It was a long time since we'd seen him looking so peaceful and contented, this certainly wasn't his normal behavior when we were late. My sister and I exchanged looks and felt puzzled.

"Fine time to come in," he remarked at last. We shuffled our feet and kept our heads down. "I think this calls for your mother's reprimand," he went on. We shot up the stairs before he could change the punishment.

What a shock we had, as we looked through the crack of the door leading to Ma's bedroom. There sat her friend by the bedside, holding an empty whisky glass, and my mother propped up with pillows, holding a shawled bundle.

"What are you standing there for?" she called out in a cheerful voice, "come and say hullo to your new sister."

THIS WAS OUR VILLAGE

Chapter Eleven

RULE BRITANNIA

"Got thee flag ready?" called out my friend Jess, racing up the garden path where I was standing cleaning my boots. She was breathless, and looked for all the world as though she'd just tumbled out of bed.

"Yer's mine," the crumpled lace pinafore was pulled out in front like a sail, and as she looked down on it I could see a tiny Union Jack, complete with stick, pinned to the gathers with a safety pin.

"Got 'im from a sherbert dab" she went on, holding up a bag with a liquorice tube poking out from the top. "Our Mam wouldn't gi'e I any money to buy a proper un. Sez Empire Day's a load of damned old rubbish."

"Well let's see thine," she ordered, holding the liquorice tube to her lips and taking a long suck that sprayed her mouth and the tip of her nose with yellow powder.

I handed her my flag, a black and white print cut from the 'Children's Newspaper', still wet from my efforts to paint red and white stripes in the right places.

"That's bloomin' good," I heard, between sucks, "All yer wants now is summat to fix down the side, so's yer can wave it." A slow smile flittered over her face as we both spotted Ma's hat, held by its bow over the back of a chair, the crown stabbed with a blue-knobbed hat pin.

We threaded it down the side of the flag and fixed the sharp end with a cork taken from an old vinegar bottle, and as the school bell gave out its final toll crossed the playground and took our places by the flagpole.

Sniffs, shufflings and nudges ceased as the Headmaster came from the main door, followed by Parson, all robed in cassock and white gown, his hands clasped as if in prayer, and a face to match the occasion.

"Attention!" shouted Bertie. Boots came together with a bang, which made a fine dust from the playground rise slowly to our knees.

Two boys walked forward to unfurl the flag. "Salute!" came the command, arms were raised and eyes looked upward, and across my piece of sky came the swirl of red, white, and blue cloth, as the flag moved lazily from the mast. "At ease." Arms dropped to sides, sniffing began again in real earnest, then to the sounds of 'The British Grenadiers' thumped out on an old piano a hundred pairs of feet marched into the main room.

We grouped ourselves around a large picture of the King and Queen hanging on a gold chain from the peeling wall, the frame draped each side with Union Jacks.

Heads bowed as Parson said a prayer, ending with the fervent request that <u>all</u> people, white, yellow or black, remember the stations that God had placed them in.

"Our Dad calls they 'chinks' and 'niggers' a boy whispered, giving his friend a nudge, their bodies moving up and down as they tittered softly. Bertie raised his cane from behind the praying priest, his stern eyes fixed on our companions, so we all decided to settle in our seats and hear what the rest of the world thought our Empire was doing.

Then came 'Rule Britannia', 'Hearts of Oak', and 'Land of Hope and Glory', sung with such fervour and fingers running up and down the piano keyboard that it completely covered the sound of the anvil being banged in the smithy across the way.

"Now to your desks," we were ordered, "I want to see the flags you've brought along."

Jess unpinned hers and laid it down on the desk with a sigh. I drew mine out of a paper bag and waited.

It took Headmaster half an hour to see them all, and we knew that only a few would be displayed on the wall later.

"Hold yours up." A boy sprang from his seat, for on a large card were fastened a set of silk cigarette cards, each one displaying a different flag.

"And you" Bertie pointed to a little girl in front of me, "come and fix yours to the wall."

"I can't" replied the girl, trembling but making no effort to move. "Mam says you can 'ave a look but I've to take it home at dinner time, 'cos that's all she's got left belonging to our Dad," her voice tailed to a whisper.

"Hold it up," his face was thunderous.

We saw a heart-shaped card edged with fine lace, two small flags, crossed, filled the center, and embroidered across the top, "To my darling wife," and underneath 'Gallipoli'[1].

At last the morning came to an end. "God save the King," we bawled, the royal picture got a second salute. "The afternoon's an official holiday" we were told, and we wasted no time in getting it.

"What about goin' round plantation and takin' some grub?" suggested Jess, as we both walked home the back way.

Ma, when she heard thought it a jolly good idea and soon filled some sugar bags with

[1] The Gallipoli campaign, Turkey, April 1915 to January 1916. After nine months of deadlock, and with the loss of 100,000 allied and Turkish soldiers, and ravaging sickness, the offensive was called off.

slices of bread and jam, gingerbread and cold sausage pasty.

As arranged, I met my friend at the top of the lane, she carried a bottle of water in one hand and an enamel milk can in the other, and dangling from her waist on a bit of binder twine, a canvas bag holding a box of matches, sugar mixed with tea in a screw of paper, and a kettle.

Down the rough road we went, passing a couple of houses belonging to a farmer, and stopped, amazed at what we saw and heard through a gate that led to a meadow.

There tethered on two ropes, a nanny goat and a baby.

"Can't watch both of they and do me work," came the angry retort from the baby's mother to her neighbour's protest about it "bein' cruel."

Past the Catholic Church and the priests bridge, and on to the farm that looked as if it had been deserted, with its tumbledown buildings, a disused forge and a black timbered barn filled with planks of wood, benches and a half-finished coffin.

"En't carryin' this lot no further," Jess was getting a bit fed up, as we reached the wide path leading into the 'plantation', so dumping our stuff behind a thick hedge, we took our boots and socks off and paddled in the small stream.

Frogs jumped high into the long grass on either side as our skirts brushed against patches of water-forget-me-not. Gurgles and bubbling sounds followed us as water tumbled over dead branches of trees and large stones.

"Whats 'ee doin' 'ere?" my friend whispered, as she stepped out of the water and pointed in the direction of the thicket. I got on to the bank and saw Young Squire dressed in plus-four trousers, thick boots and a tweed hat to match his jacket.

He was looking at a row of newly planted hazelnut trees, and seemed to be counting.

We decided to sit down on a blue carpet of periwinkles, and through a screen of beech leaves silently watched him. First he wrote something down on the long sheet in his hand, took some cuttings and put them in a canvas bag, and walked slowly to the end of the row.

A woodpecker over our heads bored into an old pine tree, and the sun made the sawdust look like gold, as it glided down softly on to our bare feet.

Young Squire moved out of sight, and we hurried back to our starting place, picking up small twigs along the way to make a fire. On the grass track, well away from the trees, I got the sticks ablaze and put the kettle on.

"Coo 'en't your Mam gi'n us some grub." Jess hauled the bags out one by one, halving the bread and jam, gingerbread and sausage pasty, and as we sat there eating and waiting for the kettle to boil I smelt the drying grass mixed with wood smoke, and clover blossom.

We'd nearly finished when three men came down the track,

"Must be knockin' off time," said the girl, "for they be carters." She got reluctantly to her feet. "S'pose us had better get back," and picking up the milk can went over to the stream and rinsed it.

I put the fire out, spread the ash with a stick, sprinkled the bare patch with some soil, and pressed it evenly with my boot.

We halted at the farm, so that Jess could get some skimmed milk.

"Mam's gunna make we a tapioca puddin' for our supper," she told the farmer's wife as she handed in the can a bit smoke-dried on the outside, and a couple of pennies.

The can was filled to the brim and returned to my friend, then we made our way slowly back homeward.

"Good old Empire Day" I shouted, giving the school flag a mock salute as we passed.

"Yer dun't believe that bloomin' rot?" Jess tossed her head. "I ben't thinkin' on that no more, not till next year," then as we reached our front door she turned, and said in a low voice, "Do yer think if yer speaks nice like to your Ma, she might gi'e I a bit more of 'er old sausage pasty?"

THIS WAS OUR VILLAGE

Chapter Twelve

CHARACTERS

"Let's cut across the common on the way back." said my sister, as we stood at the back door of the 'Gentleman Farmer's house waiting for his wife to check the rent.

This was a job given to us each week, at the end of school in the afternoon.

A small grey-haired woman returned to the kitchen, took four buns cooling on a tray and came over to the door. "That'll keep the worms from biting for a while" she said, smiling and handing us two each.

"Be careful not to lose the rent book" were

her final words as she stood watching us cross the yard, and giving a wave of her hand went inside and shut the door.

'Gleenys' seemed to be everywhere, in the cart sheds and by any open ground. Dad said the real name was guinea fowl and that they tasted better than pheasant to eat, in his opinion; I only noticed their fat speckled bodies and tiny heads and their fine legs strutting here and there.

Every building in sight was brushed, washed or painted, chicken houses and pigsties white, barns creosoted, the old cobbled yard free of litter or animal manure. It was the tidiest farm I'd ever seen.

A cockerel standing on an old water barrel, like a sentinel saw us off the premises and across the meadow.

Two horses tethered on long ropes never moved or looked up as we climbed over the gate close beside them, just kept steadily munching the soft sweet tasting grass around and making now and again little choking sounds.

We passed a long line of blackberry bushes now partly hidden by brambles, small green blackberries already formed, but it would be August before they'd be ready for picking; then with lots of our friends we'd come to gather the fruit and make a day of it picnicking.

We were talking and laughing when halfway across the common my sister suddenly stopped and with a shaking hand pointed.

There, coming towards us at a gentle pace and looking very determined, were some animals.

"Blooming bulls!" her voice rose high with alarm, we at once abandoned the usual pathway and made for a field on the right of us.

"Don't let them see that you're hurrying"

whispered my sister who was breathless. I'd got the 'stitch' something terrible in my side, and taking a furtive glance over my shoulder, noticed six fat bodies ambling towards us.

"Why haven't they got steam coming from their nostrils or foam hanging out of their mouths?" I demanded, having read about this in the story books. "'Cos you haven't any red clothes, or waving a red rag," came the answer.

A wide ditch barred our way into the field, clomping hooves could be heard getting nearer, so we both took a flying leap and landed with a thud on the other side in a heap of dead thistles.

"What's up with thee?" came a voice from the field close by, from a woman who stood watching us from one of the long rows of young turnips, her hoe idly knocking off the thistle heads as she waited for our answer.

Her companion stopped hoeing and walked

down to see for herself. Both wore thick heavy boots covered in fine dust, skirts pulled almost to their knees and fastened at the back with safety pins, the sleeves of their tight blouses were rolled up to the elbows showing strong red arms. Men's caps covered their heads and worn back to front as they worked.

"What's up?" one of them asked again, her face had a look of surprise on it.

"It's those bulls" I replied in a frightened voice, and turned to the row of brown faces on the other side of the ditch, their mouths working silently as they watched us with some interest.

"Bulls did yer say? they wouldn't 'arm a fly," the women roared with laughter, then the one nearest, seeing we hadn't believed them called out "Molly, I wun't be a minute," and came over to us.

Taking our hands in her two rough ones

she walked us close to our enemies. "See, they be milkers" she assured us. We made no reply, the woman scratched her head, looked puzzled, then had an idea. "Bend down you two" she commanded "and look at their unders."

We knelt and gave them our full attention. "Dun't ever be afraid again" the woman went on kindly "not when yer see's all they titties." We got off our knees only half believing but determined to stay with the women.

"Alright Lill?" Molly asked, then the two of them started working again on the unfinished row. Lill said something to her friend in a low voice and we heard their laughter from our thistle patch.

As they worked we tidied ourselves up, pulling the bits of grass and weeds from our coats, cleaned dust from boots, and had time to pick some wild pansies and sweet peas, whilst dark clouds moved low overhead.

Soon soft rain fell on our hair and small beadlets clung to the front of our clothes.

"Looks like settin' in for good" one of the women remarked, so they decided to finish for the day, and dropping their hoes at the end of the row covered them over with earth and a pile of weeds.

"Best cum wi us" Lill called out going over to the hedge and unrolling some sacks. They put one each around their shoulders and tossed two in our direction. We wrapped them like shawls around our heads and white powder spilled from them like snow down our coats and on to the ground.

It was a slow trudge along the narrow path by the field and out on to the main road to the village, with Molly giving out all the latest gossip and her opinion of the Gentleman Farmer.

"Ee wun't make no go of that" she said

confidently, "what wi' all 'is cleanin' and washin,' 'is 'ens dun't like it – nor do I," she gave the sack round her shoulders a vicious pull.

Lill didn't reply, she was busy holding something wrapped up in a roll of her sacking apron which I was sure I saw move each time that I gave it a sidelong glance.

Rain dripped from the women's caps on to the sacks covering their shoulders, my coat was letting in the wet and it seemed a very long time before the first of the village houses came in sight and Molly, with a cheerful "goodnight" turned up the short path home.

Lill caught me looking at her apron as we parted at the crossroads and gave me a secret smile. "If thee wants to see me new friend," her hand strayed to her apron, "better cum along to my place, arter tea."

My mother's face was a picture when we

walked in, sopping wet sacks over our heads, boots covered in mud and the rent book all smudged with blue ink, but later when we'd been rubbed dry and sat warming by the fire in our clean clothes she heard about the 'bulls' that had chased us, and how Lill had told us they were only cows and was kind enough to show us what to look for next time.

The best bit of news was left till we were all round the table eating supper. "Molly says our cottages have been sold" I told Ma, "Nobody knows yet who bought them. Molly says she's not paying any more rent to the 'Gentleman Farmer' and she thinks your'e a bloody fool if you do and that's a fact."

Ma's reaction to Molly's suggestion was totally unexpected, we were both roundly told off for repeating gossip and swear words, then sent to the kitchen to wash up the supper things.

I was sorry that I'd told Ma when several

hours later I heard her repeat the news to Dad. "I bet they'll double the rent or turn us out." she went on, and her voice sounded very worried.

******

With the washing up finished and shoes cleaned ready for school next day, I was allowed to visit Lill and her new friend.

Lill lived in one of the farm cottages close to us with her husband, known to all as 'old Alfie,' and I'd often seen him with a gang of workmen, mending the roads.

Like most of the labourers he wore cord trousers, fastened round the waist with a broad leather belt brass-buckled, string tied under each knee, and a red spotted hankie around his neck.

I don't think I ever saw him without a cap on his head or a clay pipe in his mouth. He said very little and rarely looked at anyone, yet there was not much that escaped his notice.

Tonight he was planting out lettuces in the garden, Lill standing by the pathway hanging out some washing.

"Wun't be a minute" she called as I passed close to the well. She finished pegging the clothes and brought the basket along with her.

"Thought thee was never comin," I was chided for my lateness as we walked up the short path to the wooden shed; it stood close to her front door, newly creosoted and with a window at the side.

"Ee wun't settle much tonight" my friend muttered to herself, as I heard flapping and squawking noises from inside the shed, and pressing my face close to the tiny window saw a jackdaw watching me intently with his beady eyes.

He gave a loud 'jack, jack', rose, fluttered

for a second and dropped back to the floor. Two linnets and a song thrush sat on a perch above, preening or resting with half-closed eyelids.

Lill opened the top half of the door, and bending over and with soft murmurings (unlike her usual self), lifted from the cardboard box a brown bedraggled feathered bundle. It had missing tail feathers, and only one leg.

"Cat nearly got 'in" she said, putting it into my cupped hands. I could feel the quickened heartbeat on my palms as the bird tried to snuggle in closer.

This, then, was the 'something' Lill had held rolled in her apron, when we walked back from the field before supper.

"Will it die?" I asked, looking down and hardly daring to say it.

"Not 'ee," the woman's thick fingers stroked the feathers, "an' why?, 'cos I wun't let 'in."

She took the bird from me and placed it back in the box, made soft and warm with hay and an old pair of socks belonging to her husband.

"Goodnight you lot," she bawled to the others in the shed, then shut the door and fastened it with string over a cup hanger.

"I thinks I shall call 'im Whistler" said Lill, as we walked towards the lane. Dusk had come and I could see old Alfie's shadow on the curtains in the house.

"Thank you for letting me see Whistler, can I come tomorrow?" I asked her.

"Bring some seed if thee does" she replied, knowing that Ma kept hens and always had some to spare.

What a way Lill had with birds, umpteen went into the shed for a few weeks, then I'd get a message "Come and see I let 'em out."

Some circled round her head for a while before flying off, strong and well again, others with a desperate urge to return to the wild flew straight out of her hands and away.

Only Whistler remained, living to a ripe old age, so tame that the cage was only used for sleeping or if he got a fit of the sulks.

His favourite place at dinner time was the corner of the kitchen table, balancing on his one remaining leg, daintily pecking from a dish specially prepared for him, and each spring we were repaid with birdsong from early morning until he retired at night.

Ma and I sitting in deck chairs a garden or two away could hear him, and that unmistakable voice.

Lill worked on the farm till she was over seventy, never really reconciling herself to the 'gentleman's farming', and blamed the early death of the poor man to his passion for cleanliness and order.

She proudly brought her last pay packet to show Ma. It was for ten shillings plus three shillings and sevenpence halfpenny. "What's the three and sevenpence halfpenny for?" queried Ma. "Shuttin' up they blasted 'ens" the old girl answered.

* * * * * *

Molly, her friend and workmate, on the other hand, had a different hobby. She was single and lived in a house with her widowed sister, loved the pub and its company, a mug of beer and a game of darts.

Saturdays, when the village football was in season, she'd be cheering them on or swearing at their play as she watched them.

On the day they played for the county cup she ventured far afield, a large bow of ribbon in her button-hole, and returned that night with the players on the coal lorry, which had been swept out for the occasion, and the floor lined with coconut matting.

Helped down she refused to leave till she'd kissed all the players and thanked them for "gee'n they swanky sods a good kickin'."

THIS WAS OUR VILLAGE

Chapter Thirteen

FURTHER EDUCATION

"We're bike mending tonight, girls" announced my father, coming to the doorway of the scullery, shirt collar tucked in round his neck, sleeves rolled up to his elbows, and wiping the drips from his face with a towel, as he stood waiting for our reply.

All he heard was the ticking of the clock on the mantlepiece and the sight of our scowling faces. He sighed and returned to his 'sprucing up,' leaving a strong smell of carbolic soap to mingle with the steam from a large bacon roly-poly Ma was busily unrolling from its cloth.

She slipped it on to the enamel plate warming on the stove, cheerfully ignoring our miserable looks.

"Come on" she said briskly, handing us both a tablespoon and fork, and spreading out the plates in a long line. "Let's get this dinner served up before everything's ruined."

We did as we were asked, moaning between ourselves about 'slavery to parents,' raising our voices, partly drowned by the steamer on the fire containing the rest of the meal.

"For goodness sake leave off" Ma told us when she felt we'd said enough. "What's a little puncture beside the other clever things you've learned, besides with your father's skill and your speed when you want to, it should all be over in a quarter of an hour."

I reminded her of the first gardening lesson from Pa; "one hour" he said, it had lasted the whole weekend when he found that his newly designed rake and hoe wouldn't work, and blamed it on to "those gals who didn't try hard enough."

"And what about the night we pushed the rods up the chimney" my sister joined in, keeping her eyes from looking at mine and trying not to laugh. "We did that job quick enough, and blocked our neighbour's chimney with a loose brick from the chimney pot."

Ma didn't want reminding, it had cost her two pounds of her best jam and a promise to the neighbours that she'd "get 'ee to pack up doin' what 'ee knows nothin' about."

"Go and tell your father the dinner's ready" she ordered sharply.

We fetched Pa, and everyone sat down to the table, making short work of all Ma's efforts.

It was early evening and getting dark

when Dad, pipe in hand, and with the grand air of a man who knew exactly what he wanted to achieve, gave us a long list of orders. My sister was put in charge of two lighted candles which would be the only illumination in the room. Father demonstrated how she was to hold them, raising or lowering the light over the bike wheel at his command.

I was given the task of collecting an enamel bowl and a hessian apron folded and used as a kneeling pad, and spread three tyre levers, glue, indelible pencil, patches and a tin of French chalk, on to a long wooden table.

We then set about covering the floor with old newspapers and Dad brought the bike ceremoniously in.

With a look of sheer joy on his face at the sight of his beloved machine he stood there, rubbing the flat of his hand across the saddle, then, wiping the wheels for the umpteenth time with an oily rag, turned the bike upside down with a flourish and our lesson began.

I got the tyre off and the inner tube removed, from instructions given by Pa at the top of his voice, these only ceasing when the light got moved a fraction from the job in hand, to demand "why on earth can't you keep that bloomin' candle steady."

He brought the bowl over, now half-filled with water, standing it close to the front wheel and excitedly exclaimed that there must be at least three or four holes, as bubbles thick and fast rose to the surface from the tube that had been lowered and stretched in the water.

There were three punctures, and a plopping sound as my sister dropped a candle into the bowl while responding to the shouted order to "take a good look." and bent over too far.

She was called a "fathead" and told to

"look sharp with another." She hurried out and left the door wide open, and draughts whisked the remaining light to cast dancing shadows on the wall.

We found an old torch and made a second inspection, marked the three holes with a wobbly mark and lifted the tube out of the water, patted it dry with a piece of rag, put a patch on, and liberally dusted it with French chalk.

Preparations to return the tyre to the outer rim began, confidence raised by our instructor's encouragement, and there was hardly a sound as the tyre and tube were replaced, Father thoroughly pleased with the results of his lesson.

Ma evidently felt rather uneasy with the quiet period that had overtaken us, opened the door, peeped round and quietly closed it, cups were rattled, and the saucepan taken off its hook. She was getting the supper drinks ready.

The tyre now carefully pumped up, Pa hummed a tune to himself, and thinking all was going nicely, darted over to the wall where he'd hung his coat and pulled out his tobacco pouch and pipe.

With a cry of rage which could be heard in the next street, he rushed over to the offending bike, as a long slow hissing sound came from the region of the front wheel; someone without his permission had used a tyre lever, and it had pierced the inner tube.

Half an hour later, minus one candle and the lever, Pa's opinion as to our "inability to do anything" ringing in our ears, we'd finished; the bike had been wheeled back to its special place in the shed, and we all sat around the fire drinking our cocoa.

Neither parent spoke to us, they both

seemed to be thinking, but I couldn't help hearing Dad's remark as we went up the stairs to bed,

"Never saw such a couple of slow wits," he said morosely to Ma. "Must be throwbacks from your side of the family!"

THIS WAS OUR VILLAGE

Chapter Fourteen

SUMMER TIME

The spring term at school had ended, seven glorious weeks of freedom lay ahead, and as I sat in bed watching the sun make a miniature pearl shawl of a spider's web in the opening by the window, the world seemed a lovely place again.

Gone the race to get ready for school, half eaten breakfasts, sums and history dates that to me didn't even matter, sarcasm for mistakes leaving scars that were never quite healed over the years; it was six in the morning and I was home, and on holiday.

Ma's tuneless voice floated up from the kitchen, you could tell she was concentrating for over and over the words were sung,

"If I could only plant a tiny seed of love" as she plodded between the stove and the kitchen table.

Hot fruit and sugar smells filtered up the stairs; jam making was in progress.

Every year she'd have baskets of fruit given to her, unwanted produce from many orchards round the village, and with marrow and rhubarb out of the garden and sugar at two pence a pound, Ma's enthusiasm for cooking knew no bounds.

About a hundred pots of jam would stand on the shelves, some later to be given to her friends who'd return the compliment with a swede or rabbit left on the front door steps, or perhaps a piece of pork or a comb of honey; money was the only shortage in our lives.

The day was too early to be given jobs I thought, though remembering Ma's passion for handing them out however early, I woke my sister and whispered "Let's go down to the snake pond," and soon we'd crept out of the house down the back lane.

The sun was giving warmth to our bodies, and the sky cloudless, as we moved quietly across the farmyard to the meadows, and stood in complete amazement at the scene in front of us, for the snake pond had vanished and in its place a large eye-patch of black earth and rubble.

I couldn't believe such a change could be made in such a short time, and hurried over in the direction of the running water sounds.

At the end of the old pond where the snakes used to gather, a brown pipe had been fitted to catch the spring stream, and was now busily pouring into the deep ditch newly cut and leading into another field.

There were more ditches, with small willows, like sticks, planted along them. A hedge tall and frondy divided us from the two men on the other side.

"Reckons we'd best gi'e it another stir" called the man nearest to us, as we peeped through a gap in the leaves, watching the two walk slowly up and down the wide cuts each dragging a long pole in the water.

A strong harsh smell filled the air as the poles were withdrawn showing a spoon-shaped bowl on the end. "Well, that seems to be alright" the man said to his companion, as they shouldered their spoon-poles and crossed over to the stile, leaving us with a curiosity and determination to see more, as they departed leaving the water with its smells behind.

Later that week when all the village had gone to have a quiet look we found out that the pond had been used as part of a

sewerage farm, and young Squire was told,
though only behind his back in the pub, that
it was a "damn cheek to use our snake pond
for they gentry".

Hungry, and ready for breakfast we
returned home, full of the news about the
pond and the men with their poles, and found
four jam pots filled with treacle and water
standing on the windowsill, with a plentiful
supply of wasps, dead ones floating on the
liquid and others buzzing round my mother as
she stirred the jam. "Dratted things" she said
with irritation and waving a cloth above her
head in a fruitless attempt to get rid of them.

"Sit over there," her hand pointed to the
only space left, a chair and a rickety stool by
the table.

The table was loaded with fruit in various
staged of preparation, sugar, bowls, jars, and
a weighing machine. A packet of "Sunny

Jim" cornflakes, (the latest addition from America), two dishes and spoons, and of course umpteen pots of jam.

In front of me was a large cream-coloured jug, painted on one side of it the head of Lord Kitchener, the face a bright red with pin-point eyes and a waxed moustache and on the other side when you turned it round, two coloured flags; the milk inside the jug was protected from the flies by a net doily edged with multi-coloured beads.

We were given a dish of cereal, and later a glass of lemonade. Ma's duty to us finished she turned back to her cooking and promptly forgot us.

Sitting at the table and swinging my foot, I watched the baker and his daughter delivering bread along the row of houses, his small two-wheeled covered handcart now resting on its weighted legs at the back, whilst the man filled his basket with bread and cakes. Short and jolly, dressed in a coarse tweed suit, he'd walk round the village close to the Downs selling his wares, the bakery and small shop not far from the turnpike a very hive of industry seven days of the week.

Sunday he cooked some of the villagers' midday meal, a large meat tin with a joint sitting in the middle, surrounded with potatoes and parsnips. The uncooked dinner was taken by the men on their way to the allotment or pub, and collected a few hours later, steaming hot and wrapped in a white cloth.

Now the baker had reached our door, with two loaves of bread and a lardy cake.

Ma paid him and he gave me a bag of striped peppermint humbugs, next week perhaps the present would be a tiny cottage loaf, crusty and so tiny that it could sit in the palm of my hand.

The morning was nearly over and my mother was on the last batch of fruit, picking it over and weighing out the sugar, when my brother and his friend appeared.

"Ma, we're going to 'shock up' the corn in the field at the back, and we won't have time to come in and have our dinner properly." He turned, saw us and said casually, "if you kids bring some food along later, we'll let you stay."

I was about to protest when I noticed his feet. This thirteen year old was wearing a dainty pair of lace boots, and his legs wrapped in putties belonging to my father; a compromise to this morning's argument between my parents.

"Hobnailed boots" said Pa "were the right footwear for the job."

"You're making a navvy out of him" my mother protested; dainty boots won, but not before putties were mentioned as the 'right gear' by Dad, and accepted by both Ma and wearer.

Around dinner time we set out for the field, my sister holding two bottles of cold tea and me carrying a bag filled with sandwiches.

Several men were busy with scythes, cutting a wide band of corn all around the outside of the field ready for the reaping to begin.

I could see my brother and his friend holding the horses steady at the far end of the field, and a man with trouser bottoms tied with string sat on the metal seat of the machine, waiting.

Scything finished, the reins were pulled with a jerk, horses and reaper began to move round and round the field, ripe corn cut clean with flails fixed over the cutter, later to be thrown out in neat sheaves from the side of the machine to the ground.

Young boys and women followed on foot, picking up the sheaves and stacking them like small wigwams on the stubble to dry.

There were many shouts, swearwords, "hold there" and "steady Bessy"s, before the field was partly finished and a halt called for food.

One man clubbed a rabbit as it was making for the hedge, and a boy eager to pick it up got his foot caught in a scythe.

He was carried to the edge of the field and laid down on an old sack, the wound bound with a cloth taken from the sweating neck of one of the workers.

He was told to "bide quiet for a bit," and a woman went over to him. "Silly young varmint" we heard as she unscrewed a bottle of tea and passed it to the boy to drink, he took a good swig, wiped the top of the bottle with his hand and returned it, then everybody found a place in the shade under the hedge. The carter put nosebags on the horses, and we all settled down for an hour.

Men and women opened red spotted handkerchiefs, pulling out loaves cut in half, slabs of cheese, and whacking great onions which they cut into pieces with a very sharp knife and directed it skilfully to their mouths without cutting themselves.

We youngsters exchanged bread and jam for slices spread liberally with pigs lard and smothered with brown sugar, our fruit cake for lumps of 'lardy', and cold tea for murky 'bee wine'.

Stretched out full length on the ground and only half listening, we heard scraps of news from the grown-ups;

"They be goin' to tar top road for the fust time next spring" said one.

"A waste o' good money" his companion

replied, and was told "Dun't be a silly bugger, thee knows 'twill be more work for thy Ted."

The sun was giving us a belting. I looked round for more shade. "Go and sit in old Siffy's house" suggested one of the women and laughed heartily at the idea, for Siffy and his brother Eli were tramps wandering from workhouse to workhouse.

They always made a point of visiting our village in the spring, making a shelter close to the field we were sitting in.

It consisted of three bales of straw, one each side and the other perched on top, pushed well into the hedge to avoid the wind.

Siffy and Eli always paid a visit to the school, waiting outside the playground for their tidbits; bites of apple, tomato, half buns and cold sausage, which they wrapped carefully into an old rag and stuffed into their pockets.

For a week, perhaps, we'd see them, billycans and a canvas bag tied round their middles with a length of string, feet in boots bound with rags, then they'd vanish till the spring came again, leaving the shelter to the rabbits and other wild creatures.

My sister and I decided to share it as the workers got up to start 'shucking' again, and by seven that night the job was finished and the field covered with wigwams of sheaves, standing in long, straight rows.

The men and women, tired and dusty trudged off down the road, my brother and his friend astride the two horses led by the carter.

Ma's jam-making session had finished by the time we reached home, the table cleared and scrubbed and rows of jars filled to the brim, paper-capped and labelled.

We told her of our adventures, about the rabbit that had been clubbed, and the boy who cut his foot; but her face changed like the weather when we reached the 'Siffy house' part of the story.

Smiles went out and an angry look took its place, we were ordered to the shed and stripped of the few clothes we had on, a bowl was filled with warm water and some paraffin, a flannel and large bar of washing soap held at the ready.

First came a thorough going over with the paraffin mixture in the bowl, a bath with soap and nailbrush treatment, then, hair in bobbles and draped in our nightclothes, we were allowed to the table, my hunger by that time too big to be satisfied by one meal.

Ma sat there, her face still in the stormy quarter but she must have relented a bit, for by each plate stood a paste pot that had been washed out and filled with jam, and with a crinkly paper cap, and labelled like the big ones with our names, in bold lettering round the middle.

THIS WAS OUR VILLAGE

Chapter Fifteen

DUTY WORK AND OUTINGS

During the winter my brother had joined the Scouts, a new troop started up by an old Major living in the village.

For several weeks he wore his ordinary clothes, with only a green garter tab pushed into the turnover of his sock to show that he'd been allowed to join.

One evening he returned in full dress uniform: khaki shirt with two square chest pockets, a matching pair of cotton shorts baggy and ending at the knees, and a scout hat, broad-brimmed and the crown like a pudding basin that had been dented in three places meeting at the top in a small point. It was held firmly in place on the head with a fine brown leather chinstrap.

"How do I look, Ma?" he said, turning around slowly so that we could all see the tin mug on a small ring on one side of the belt around his waist, whistle and jackknife on the other.

My mother's face filled with pleasure and pride, and so did my brother's but for a very different reason.

"See this" he said, picking up a stout wooden pole from the chair where he'd put it on coming in. "I can't think why you want that" Ma's voice sounded a bit indignant, she was probably thinking of the price it had all come to.

"Come and watch me," he shot over to the doorway, and pressing with both hands on the upright stick swung himself easily over a small fence into the garden.

"That's what you do when you want to get over a waterhole or an obstacle" he informed her, "Baden Powell's doing it all the time.

"He's our Leader you know but we haven't seen him yet. Next year when he comes to the Jamboree I'll have a good look."

Over the next month my sister and I joined the Scouts (unofficially of course) and were pushed into straight lines in our back garden, given impossible instructions by a miniature Scout Master, followed by endless saluting, reef knot tying and whittling of tent pegs; whilst blisters on our hands came and went by the dozen.

There was some slight unpleasantness between the farmer and our family over the initials ATK appearing overnight on the barn door in the rickyard, and things came to a sharp halt after a week of whistle blasts at six a.m. from the new scout's bedroom window calling us on parade. The 'old soldier' (my father) had had enough.

Things quieted down until summer came, when a camp was held for a week on the Downs.

Several days were spent at home, raising and lowering the tent, learning how to knock tent pegs in correctly and sorting out the oldest knife, fork and spoon. The last job was easy seeing that there was nothing but old stuff in our house, and on one Friday night we waved him off, a canvas bag stuffed to the brim on his shoulders, mug and billycan hanging from his waist and carrying the pole that went everywhere with him.

Teatime the following Saturday they returned. My father was cleaning his boots in the shed and called out "They're turning into the lane, all the bloomin' lot of 'em."

We could hear "Pack up your troubles" sung by out of tune voices, and the uneven tramp of feet, ending with a loud "Halt" at our front door.

The Scoutmaster saluted Ma and my brother stepped out from behind him, there was more saluting then the rest of the pack, headed by its leader, departed.

He stood there on the doorstep, eyes bright as buttons, a huge smile on his face black-smutted from all the camp fires he'd tended, hair that hadn't been brushed for a very long time and one shoe burnt away at the toe showing a sock hanging out at the end.

Ma welcomed him home like the prodigal son, there was no ranting on about his appearance, she just ruffled his hair, told him tea was nearly ready, and that she was glad he'd enjoyed himself so much.

My father who'd been watching from the back door returned to his cleaning, thoroughly disillusioned at the sight he'd seen.

"That Major's a phoney" we heard him say to himself. "No real soldier would allow a boy to come home in that state, no never" he repeated, brushing his highly polished boots with more vigour.

Ma told Dad later on that camps were places that people went to for enjoyment, and after all it was only for a week. Pa made no answer but ever after, referred to the scoutmaster as "The Phoney Major."

* * * * * * * * *

It was the Major however who unwittingly contributed to my first real outing; the seaside, when on his retirement from the service he decided to devote his energies to a fruit farm.

At the time of the scout episode he'd

already a fine apple orchard in the village,
stretching from the bakehouse to the turnpike,
and currant bushes planted in the spare
ground between the trees where ripe fruit was
waiting to be picked.

Ma's friend who we called 'Auntie',
gave out the news that currant pickers were
wanted at this fruit farm, when she came for
a gossip with Ma one evening, a large brown
china teapot, cups and a plate of buns sitting
on the table between them.

The village scandal was picked over for
a good quarter of an hour, whilst we hung
about in the background listening to what
they had to say, as we stretched out the last
hour before bedtime.

"Do you remember when we worked at
Knole?" said Auntie, who had no intention
of departing yet.

Of course Ma remembered, once again

holding out her deformed feet for inspection,
and reminded all her listeners that that
was the result of hours spent standing on hot
kitchen floors, cooking for hundreds of people.
Auntie chimed in and displayed a long scar
on her hand that she'd received from the chef
when he'd had "one of his fits on."

Then we heard of the gentry, 'real people'
Ma called them. They must have been for they
seemed to have enjoyed themselves immensely;
there was a Duke and his mistress, a Duchess
and her 'good friend' who appeared to be rather
'special'.

Auntie didn't give his name but he was
rather stout, wore a grey beard and could do
or say just as he pleased as "there was none
higher in the land." she went on.

"Real people they certainly were," Ma's
voice took on a proud note as she handed the
buns round, "even if they thought we knew

Duty Work and Outings

nothing about the way they went on."

Both were silent for a second then recollections of the antics of 'the rich ones' at Knole sent them both into peals of laughter.

Ma was back to the chef story, told for the umpteenth time at these get-togethers which she loved to have now and again.

"Do you know, that old chef expected me to start work at four in the morning, however late I'd worked through the evening, and once sent a kitchen maid to my bedroom with a message, "Was Madam intending to stay there all day"? when I happened to be a quarter of an hour late, and all for eight bob a week." The two friends sighed and put their cups down.

Every bun on the plate gone and the teapot nearly emptied, they ended the conversation with the set piece we all remembered, how strange that fate had brought them together again after such a long time, and that it showed that wars not only parted friends but reunited.

'Twas getting dark. Ma got up and fetched the oil lamp, lit it and adjusted the wick. She had some news of her own to impart, "Arth's at last been offered a job," she almost whispered it to her friend as though she couldn't yet believe it.

"At the Depot? I heard they were opening it to ex-service men" said Auntie, going over to Mum and giving her a hug.

"Well this really calls for a celebration" went on the woman, rummaging through her hessian bag and drawing out a bottle of stout.

"I was going to have this with my supper but never mind, go on one of you girls and get us a couple of glasses."

They were brought in and polished whilst she sat talking to Ma.

"Just fancy, three years unemployment

for an ex-soldier. That's your blasted country's gratitude for you I must say," she poured the brown liquid into the glasses, they raised them, said "three cheers" and drank.

Ma, overcome with it all dabbed her eyes with her hankie, just as Auntie put the empty bottle in my hand. "You can get a penny on this tomorrow if you take it to the Jug and Bottle department, dear."

Without a word the bottle was taken from me by my mother and returned to her friend's hessian bag.

Dad returned from the allotment before our visitor had departed and the new job was discussed once again. Finally, with every bit of news rung out, scandal at an end, Auntie picked her bag up and got as far as the door.

The most interesting news for us was given as one foot hovered over the threshold,

"Did you know they're getting up an

outing to Weston-Super-Mare in a fortnight's time?" we were asked, "Your girls can come with me if they like, ten bob each person." she called out half way down the path.

"Thanks" Pa called out and slammed the door.

****

That night I thought about Weston-Super-Mare, and a ride in the train, donkey rides and paddling, and it wasn't until morning when I awoke, that I remembered if I wanted to go I'd have to find ten shillings.

I needn't have worried for the problem was solved for me when I met my school friends.

"We'em goin' currant pickin' tonight" they told me, "thee cum' we us to old Major's orchard".

I was only too pleased to, and about a dozen children including me arrived at the fruit farm just after five o-clock.

For a short time we stood silently waiting outside the closed gate. No one came. A boy shouted through the fence "Open up can't yer," the foreman walked from the shed across the small yard, looked us over, checked his watch and went back inside.

Eventually everything must have been ready for he returned and unlocked the gate, we swarmed in like bees where the women stood busily packing fruit for market, pushing and shoving to be first to get our baskets.

In a long line we waited whilst the flat cardboard shapes were folded into baskets and given one to each with instructions about the picking.

"I wants no stones, grit or stalk when yer brings 'em back in," then like prisoners we were led into the warm, sunlit field, and given a row to get started on.

Black fruit hung in clusters on bushes

which seemed to stretch for miles. There was a sharp smell from crushed overripe currants that had fallen to the ground. I bent down and started to pick the fruit as fast as I could. There wasn't a sound from my part of the field, only men's voices and turning cartwheels going along the turnpike road.

Two hours later, with aching back and fruit piled high in the basket, I returned to the shed for the weighing.

Getting all the fruit sorted out took a very long time, with the foreman giving us his opinion about our work as stones stalks and green leaves came to light.

It was my turn at last to put a basket on the scales. The weights could be adjusted to fourteen pounds, mine went down at six, I was handed sixpence and thanked for coming along.

Passing through the packing yard that

night, I gave silent thanks to the 'phoney Major' who'd made my wealth possible, and if my luck held and the fruit lasted out, I'd certainly be going with 'Auntie', to the outing.

****

Well it didn't, and four days before the trip to the seaside was due, still short of a shilling I sat swinging my legs on the churchyard wall, waiting for a miracle to happen. And it came in the shape of a weedy seventeen year old youth, known to everyone as Nobby.

He was ginger-haired, freckled and had a nervous twitch, and with only one sound eye, having lost the other in an accident. Everyone felt sorry for Nobby and his misfortune, and had clubbed round for the price of a glass one.

Spruced up in his Sunday suit he'd

come along to show it to his friends, and in the best of moods leaned against the church wall, waiting, the tail end of a Woodbine hanging from the corner of his mouth, and another in his shaking hand, at the ready to pop in.

Youths turned up in dribs and drabs, some on bikes, others walking. Nobby was the centre of their attention for a while, taking out the glass eye, rubbing it on his shirt cuff, and showing it round.

Soon the talk drifted to Dempsey and his boxing. Arguments started about the next fight, a gypsy looking lad put his fists up, somebody made a lunge, missed the intended victim and hit our ginger friend knocking him out cold on to the ground.

Minutes later he sat up minus his glass eye, looking as green as the grass he was sitting on; there was a mad scramble to find it whilst the owner got up and leaned over the wall, recovering.

After a long unfruitful search they left him, with promises of "havin' another whip round, Nobb, to get thee another one."

The grass now well flattened and daylight fading fast, it was time for me to go home, and when I told Dad all about Nobby and his eye, he said "Twas a bloomin' shame and we'd both go and have a look in the morning."

I found it next day near the path, after Pa had put the billhook over the grass and we'd raked it thoroughly, none the worse for a night laying on a worm mound.

Wiped clean and placed on a piece of cotton wool in a matchbox, we took it round to the gardens where Nobby worked, and on the following morning by my breakfast plate was a crumpled Woodbine packet, inside a shilling and a note. "Thanks for my eye, yers a bob for thee trouble. Nobby!"

Dad said "'Twas a miracle finding that bit of glass," I thought getting the shilling for my outing was another.

****

Eight o-clock on a humid summer morning, still with a hint of rain from the night before, I knocked on Auntie's door and a cheery voice called out "Come on in," and I saw Ma's friend doing battle with a long hat pin through the straw hat, perched at an angle on her head.

There was a quick straightening of the hair fringe, and a brushing of invisible spots off her coat, then with a quick wave to her husband standing moodily at the gate, we hurried up the street to meet the others.

Outside the sweet shop several women and

children waited, and on catching sight of us, one of them, a large bundle of Macintosh, brown felt hat and galoshes, separated herself from the crowd.

"Now we are all here," she said, looking at us with contempt for being late, "we'll make a start and hope the train will be late," then slammed open a man's black umbrella over her head and strode to the head of the party.

"Silly bitch" said a young woman without malice, who was holding a tiny baby in her arms and with us trailed further behind as the pace increased, on the two mile walk to the station.

It took ten minutes to cover the turnpike road and turn left on to one of the most potholed tracks in Berkshire, called Feather Bed Lane, sliding like worms to avoid holes and mud, coming out later onto firmer ground, bedraggled and on the wrong side of the railway line.

"Signal's down," shouted a boy and everyone started to run, reaching the platform as the train puffed in filling everywhere with steam and smoke.

"Excursion to Weston-Super-Mare," the porter's voice rang out, "last stop before Weston."

We stood in a group whilst names were checked against a list in the pudgy hand of our leader. The porter, satisfied, allowed us to board, a whistle blew, and we were off on our journey.

It was already packed with bucket and spade waving toddlers, fretful Mums and weary Dads carrying bags of sandwiches. There was shin kicking and groaning before everyone had settled, the train already well on its way to the seaside.

For a long time we amused ourselves,

watching the countryside fly past the window, and racing along to a small cubicle marked 'Toilet' at the end of the corridor. "Dun't 'alf jolt yer" said a small girl "when yer sittin' on that little seat, 'specially when yer crosses they lines," she patted her bottom.

I was busy tucking in to the sandwiches Ma had given me for my dinner, and occasionally trying to read the back of the church magazine old 'Galoshes' was reading.

After what seemed to me a very long time, when children were tired of shouting and eating, the grown-ups started to gather up their belongings and we steamed into Weston-Super-Mare station.

The platform was crowded with people, all determined to be first past the ticket collector.

"Don't forget to be back here by six o-clock," reminded our voice of authority for the third time, then the party split into groups, 'Galoshes' coming with 'Auntie' and several of us children, everybody following the sign pointing to the sea.

At the bottom of the street we turned right, following a strong smell that we were told was the 'ozone'.

"Well I'm blowed" said Ma's friend, as a whelk stall and a few donkeys stood where the sea should have been. "Fancy that." She looked at her companion darkly for the failure of the sparkling foam.

"They never told me that the tide would be out today when I bought the tickets" answered the woman, quivering with indignation and disappointment.

'Auntie' was satisfied with the explanation, besides, now she could be on Christian name terms with her 'companion', whom she felt was unreliable.

"Never mind, Milly," 'Auntie's voice was

patronising, "If it's in tonight we can have a paddle but now if you don't mind we'll start the present buying." Milly humbly agreed and they moved on.

The first shop on the front had a large window filled with sticks of rock, crest china, and mugs with the words "For my old man" written in gold lettering on the side, fancy hats and ticklers, buckets and spades, shells, and postcards of fat ladies bathing or sprawling in bright bloomers on the sands.

Outside the shop across a pathway on the edge of the mud-coloured sand was a galvanised shed, and standing by it a tough looking man in seaman's jersey, and trousers rolled up to the knees.

He was dropping grey crabs into a copper of boiling water in front of him and drawing them out when they changed to red. Close by his elbow, on a stand a notice read, "fresh crabs, cooked while you wait, two shillings each please."

Milly bought one. "That'll do for Dad's tea tomorrow." It was wrapped in newspaper and pushed to the bottom of her bag, together with four sticks of rock, winkles, and a nice bit of crest china.

We had donkey rides and I fell off, got picked up and sitting on it backwards got photographed, balloon chasing, and making sand castles as we waited for the sea to return. It never did so the outing ended with putting socks and shoes on over gritty feet.

"Think we'll go and find something to warm us up" Auntie suggested. Milly agreed with eagerness and ordered everyone to "Keep a sharp look out for a drinking place" and with eight pairs of eyes and not much running about we soon found a place for refreshment.

Our two grown up friends disappeared into

the Jug and Bottle department, returning a few minutes later with glasses of lemonade and a packet of biscuits between the six of us, then feeling they'd done their bit, settled themselves in a couple of chairs by the door, and sat contentedly sipping the pale looking liquid from two tiny glasses.

At six-fifteen we were the first group to return to the station, so that we could sit together, and just before the train was due to depart the others came straggling in.

Whilst babies slept on mothers laps, presents and postcards where shown around; someone started a sing song and paper hats were put on, there were riddle-me-rees and jokes bandied about.

'Auntie', flushed with excitement and stout, sang "The end of a perfect Day" and it lasted until our station came in view, ending abruptly with someone standing on her feet as the train came to a halt, and the scramble to get on to the platform began.

Our 'Leader' (Milly) from early morning, paper hat still perched on her felt hat, decided that her job was finished. "You all know the way home, so I'll leave you to it," and by the time everyone had reached the village and said goodnight, the moon shone like a great silver ball in the sky.

Ma asked me if I liked the sea and seemed puzzled when I said I didn't trust it, but if she'd asked me did I enjoy the outing, that would have been different and my answer: yes, yes, every minute.

THIS WAS OUR VILLAGE

Chapter Sixteen

AUTOMOBILES

What excitement there seemed to be in the village this morning I thought, as my sister and I stood on the high bank opposite a row of houses bustling with activity.

We were returning from an early walk on the Downs and we each wore a necklet of string hung with small yellow bobbles; cowslips gathered whilst the dew still clung to them and now made into cowslip balls.

Steam rose from our soaking wet boots and the edges of our dresses, as we leaned in the warm sun on the railings, watching with great interest the comings and goings across the road separating us.

A boy came over, dressed in a sailor suit, boots, and what appeared to be a small fitting cap, but as he scaled the bank I could see that his hair had been shorn all over, to about half an inch from his head.

"Our lot's goin' to Wembley to Ex'bition," he told us.

"Our Mam sez whether I likes it or not I be sittin' on 'er lap all the way so I goes free in that old charabang."

He swung over and over on the bar between the railings until he was spotted by his father.

"Cum on yer and gi'e I a 'and" shouted the harassed man, trying to tie a very fat baby into a canvas pushchair. The boy returned and was promptly given the baby to mind and a large paper bag filled with something.

Neighbours on either side came out, everyone dressed in their Sunday best, doors were locked, and glances given all round before the door-key was slipped under a mat or flowerpot.

The boy's parents were the last to leave, the pushchair wheel seemed to be the difficulty, and as they hurried up the road we followed, anxious to see this thing called a 'charabang' that the boy had talked about.

A large crowd had already gathered outside the public house when we arrived, everyone talking nineteen to the dozen, women only stopping in their chatter to tell the men-folk "Can't thee just for once look arter our Bert, 'ee's makin' a gert 'ole in 'is jacket" or, "Dun't thee get so impatient, man, chara' wun't cum no quicker for thy moanin'."

At last the sound of the horn was heard,

all heads turned in one direction, and a hushed crowd watched the charabang roll majestically into view finally halting close beside us.

We pressed forward and saw a long, rounded, black-painted body with a canvas covered hood, white rimmed wheels and a lovely brass horn. It stood so high from the ground that a rubber-covered platform had been fixed along the bottom, and there were several brass-handled doors along the side.

A rather important looking man sat at the driving wheel, and as the charabang stopped he opened his cab door and waited for a few seconds studying the list in his hand, whilst we all looked up at him expectantly.

He stepped carefully down, opened each door in turn and for the first time pretended to notice us.

One by one names were called out from the

sheet held in his hand, excitement mounting as people began slowly to climb in. Dads, Mums, kids and bags of all sizes and shapes got fitted in five abreast, along the padded seats.

"That's the lot then," said the driver importantly, putting the last tick to the paper and pushing it into his pocket.

"No 'taint, we en't got our organiser yet," shouted a woman from the back. "No good goin' wi'out she," the voice went on, "we dun't know where Wembley is."

Just at that moment one of the men leaned over the side of the charabang, and caught his son rubbing the bodywork with his jersey sleeve.

"Get thee blasted 'ands off and go and see if she's cummin," he told the lad irritably, "and you wave when she gets to the corner so we can tell driver to get steam up."

The boy, red faced and sheepish at being

told off in front of his friends, shot off down the road on his errand, whilst the waiting occupants tried to decide "what made 'er allus late on important occasions."

At the corner the boy waved and the driver started the engine up, everybody began issuing instructions.

"Dun't ferget to give our Gramp his dinner."

"Shut they 'ens up at six o-clock sharp," and "Mind thee be'aves theeself till I gets 'ome," the last remark embracing all who stood there waiting to see them off.

The organizer reached the charabang, powdered, rouged, and breathless, her straw hat only just held on by a motoring veil, the latter being vainly retied with hands that held two crochet bags and an umbrella.

Lifting up her long white motoring coat she put one cream stocking'd leg ending in a red shoe on the running board, and was unceremoniously pushed into a seat by the driver, who seemed deaf to her genteel apologies for her lateness.

Cheers rose from all sides as the vehicle started to move, together with arm waving and blown kisses, till it disappeared round the bend of the road, and the noise of the engine died away.

* * * * * *

"Wish I could 'ave gone to Wembley" said a girl called Jess, joining my sister and I with her brother as we crossed the meadow leading back home.

"Stop thee grizzlin' and come and 'ave a look at this," he held in his hand a small egg. "Belonged to a sparrer," he informed us, "and if yer promises not to split I'll show yer the nest where it came from."

The egg was passed from his hand to ours,

it felt warm, fragile, and looked beautiful, then silently we were led to the hedge and in the thickest part of it saw a round circle of grass and moss with three eggs sitting in the middle.

The boy placed a small stone beside them, "That's so she wun't miss the one I took" he told us confidently, and wrapping the egg in a couple of dock leaves put it carefully into his pocket.

Jess and I stopped to pick bunches of milkmaids and buttercups for our mothers as the boy, twirling his cap round and round in his hand, wandered to the smithy.

It was warm. We sat down leaning our backs against a log, and watched soft lazy clouds make cotton wool pictures across the sky, hearing the even beat of hammer on anvil and cuckoo song in the distance.

"Jess, where be you?" came an urgent

voice, boots crunching on gravel getting closer.

"I'm yer," she bawled, holding her hand high above the grass. There were two strong sniffs as he bent over us.

"You knows that old painter gel" said the boy, "the one wi' bobbed 'air, 'oo smokes like a chimney, well – she's gunna give a ride in that old car of 'ern to any on us who'll sit for one of 'er paintin's."

"Dun't tell lies our Tom" replied the girl, getting up and giving him a push with her hand. "She 'ad us sittin' all arternoon at school last year, while she painted and not one thing did she gi'e us."

"Our Mam said you couldn't tell t'other from which child, when she see'd it 'angin' in the classroom."

Despite Jess's protests it was clear the car ride was an attraction, we got up and slowly walked past the smithy and joined with three other girls who were offering their services, and soon stood on the artist's doorstep, lifting the knocker.

It was answered by a tall youngish looking woman in a paint-stained smock covering a tartan skirt, unruly bright red hair plaited into a big flat bun at the back, but it was her eyes that attracted me most; large, grey-green with ginger lashes.

These were gazing at me now for I stood nearest and nobody had told her what we wanted.

"Yes?" her face took on a half smile, I lost my voice and Tom (the smallest) became our spokesman.

"Please Miss, we've come to sit for the paintin'," then noticing the older woman partly hidden by the curtain, "it's she we wants." His grubby finger pointed to the occupant behind her.

The tall woman turned and I saw her

face reflected in the mirror for a half second, it held a broad smile and in a shaky voice she called out "Margaret, you have some visitors waiting for you."

She moved away and then I knew that the car ride could never be ours — but surely that mirror was lying, those five girls in faded patched up dresses couldn't be us with white-toed boots and not a ribbon between us. Or Tom, hands firmly planted in the pockets of his ragged trousers, cap on top of ears, lips pursed, waiting for an answer.

The old 'Painter gel' came and surveyed us thoughtfully, a paint-smeared finger stroking her chin.

"I think I'll accept everyone of you," she said very businesslike, and shook our hands solemnly. "Gentleman's agreement" we were told.

"When be we getting' the ride?" Tom at

least hadn't forgotten what we came for.

"Half past two today" I heard as if in a dream and the door was shut quietly behind us.

That afternoon, with boots cleaned and best dresses on, manners freshened up from a long rigmarole given by Ma we stood once again pounding the knocker. It was answered almost at once by the tall lady we'd seen in the morning, who now wore a tartan jacket and a matching hat decorated with small green feathers.

As we stood there the car drew up to the door, I'd never seen such a posh one, long sleek body with lots of brass handles. The top was open as the large pram-like hood had been fixed down secure at the back, and held by two shiny buttons.

A man in grey uniform, black riding gloves and highly polished gaiters climbed out of the driving seat, hurried round to open the door by the back seat and told us children to climb in. Two seconds it took us to get sorted out and inspect the little pockets on each side of the polished padding.

Then the door to the front seats was opened and the uniformed man saluted and helped the ladies in.

Margaret our painter friend wore no hat and only a crochet shawl round her shoulders.

We waited with impatience as a large wicker basket (like Squire used for his laundry) was strapped on to the metal rack across the back of the car and at last, as everything seemed to be ready the driver got in and started up.

"Bettr'n old chara" Jess said, leaning over and watching the road whizz past as we sped along the turnpike. I sat back and watched the green fields on either side spreading into the distance like long silk scarves, hedges of scented May, borders of Queen-Anne lace, conker flowers, and tassles of laburnum.

At last the village came in sight and the car parked outside a very large house by the arm of the river.

Everyone scrambled out kicking the paintwork, the uniformed man looked on with great displeasure, but his scowls turned to smiles when his employer suggested that he had an hour off at the 'Green Man' for his lunch, and to send the bill in to her for payment, then telling us to follow her along the towpath, lit up a cigarette in a long holder and strode out.

Amazed at such behaviour, like sheep we walked along the broad ribbon of a path leading to a bridge spanning the water. On one side the smooth river was close to our feet and so clear that the weeds could be seen hugging the bottom.

There was a mighty roar under the bridge as a wheel fixed to some machinery on the bank was turned and water released to tumble several feet into a lake and join with the river further down.

We saw moorhens, swans and cygnets, punts and skiffs, summer-houses with thatched roofs and great lumps of frothy brown scum that our artist's friend called 'giant sponges'.

Sticks were thrown over the side of the next bridge, there was a rush to the other side to see who was the winner, a bag of striped cloves came our way followed by turkish delight, and all the time cigarettes were smoked and new ones immediately replaced in the long holder.

"Now, wish" said our hostess throwing wide her arms as though embracing the whirlpool, "If you close your eyes and wish hard King River will come up and greet you."

"All I wants is me tea" said Tom, he was promptly pulled out of earshot by Jessie.

"Yer knows what our Gramp said when 'ee 'eard we wuz goin', yer got to go along wi' the old woman even though we knows she ain't right – well then wish likes she asked" Jess said and he was given a mighty push when he repeated that he felt "bloomin' 'ungry."

The path ended in a green track leading to a field covered in buttercups and daises and there we found the chauffeur with the wicker basket. It was opened by the lady with the green eyes, and the cloth laid out.

"Help yourselves" came the invitation, and we didn't waste any time. There were sandwiches by the score, cakes and jelly. Ma would have been surprised if she'd seen how we ate and played games of 'I spy' all at the same time.

As the last cake and sandwich vanished

plates were wiped off with grass and neatly stacked away, then followed games of tag, three-legged races and running to the gate for prizes of chocolates and jelly babies.

It was time to return. All stood by the bridge for a last look, long sprays from the whirlpool reached up and kissed us, then we moved away, hearing the muted sound of water being carried along sending out smells of silt, weeds, and marsh plants.

We changed seats for the journey back. except the ladies who were helped in by the man in grey.

"Are we going the long way home?" Tom asked hopefully, as the car was guided left this time instead of going through the village.

The road led to an old stone bridge with a tiny house built on to the side, and outside the front door stood a man with a cash bag slung across his chest. He held his hand up and the car halted beside him.

"Threepence toll, Sir," his voice most respectful to our driver who had the money tucked in a small leather purse neatly fixed inside the windscreen. The ticket was issued, the ladies bowed and got a hat raised in their direction.

"Varmints!" he mouthed silently to us as we swept a deeper bow to him, in our efforts to be as polite as those in front.

We sang 'Old Lang Syne' and 'Cherry Ripe,' 'Haul the Bowline' and 'Scotland for Ever.' The lady in the tartan suit said she liked the last one best of all so we sang her another couple of lines with great gusto.

Men were returning from work on their bikes and women stood at their gates waiting as we swung round the corner by the memorial and drew up in great style by the painter's front garden.

There was "Thank you, Miss," Tom

saluted and one of the girls curtsied as we turned to go.

"Haven't you forgotten something?" the painter's voice ran out loud and clear. We stopped dead in our tracks and came back.

"See you tomorrow at half past nine for the painting," a smoke-stained finger pointing in our direction. "Remember we all shook hands this morning, and that," her voice held a mocking tone, " – was a gentleman's agreement."

THIS WAS OUR VILLAGE

Chapter Seventeen

THE FETE

"Dun't put any of they old thistles in thy pot" said my friend, taking a close look at the wild flowers I was arranging, and checking them against her own.

"If they judges pricks their fingers on 'em tomorrow yer wun't get no prize that's for sure," she warned.

The offending flowers were pulled out and some tottle grass, heavy with pollen, added for I really did want to collect the gold edged card and the half-crown prize that went with it.

Tonight all the village was getting ready for the fete to be held in the park, by kind permission of Squire's widow, who would open it "at two thirty prompt," well that's what the notice on the barn said.

Ma had shut herself in the kitchen, window and door tightly closed against the draughts; sounds of wooden spoon on bowl, her droning song and hot cake smells drifted now and again through the gap in the worn threshold.

"Our Dad's gunna put a mark on all 'is show beans this year," I heard, my thoughts snatched from the kitchen and Ma's efforts. "And the plate they stands on," Liz my friend continued, "'cos 'ee reckons they judges mixed 'is lot up wi' the bloke 'oo won first prize, so 'ee's makin' sure it dun't 'appen this time."

The girl picked another flower from the pile and rammed it in the overflowing jam pot, wiped the bottom with a corner of her apron and stood it on the copper in the cool shed.

"Just look at that marrer!" she exclaimed, coming from the shed into the light again, making sure her voice carried two doors away where a youth with rolled up sleeves and a perpetual smile stood rubbing the shiny green skin gently with lard on a piece of rag.

"E'nt 'ee a whopper?" Liz walked up to the lad, "must be all that pigs muck yer puts on it" she teased him.

"Clear off!" came a voice from a capped head at the window, "And you, Barney," he bawled to the boy, "you've polished that damned thing long enough. Cum on in and gi'e I a 'and with these 'taters."

Daylight was fading before the last barrow and truck had been loaded, then covered with sacks and trundled into shed or kitchen for safety till the next day.

My friend collected her flowers, cradling the jar in one arm and, slowly munching a piece of sugary bread pudding Ma had given her, departed for home.

* * * * *

Long before ten o'clock the next morning Dad and I joined the crowd all making their way through the park to the big tent, each exhibit carefully wrapped in paper bag, pillowcase or well-washed sack so that his neighbour wouldn't see and take advantage.

They were halted sharply at the tent opening by a man, looking very important in pin-striped suit and trilby hat drooped over one eye, who passed us in one by one with a delicate wave of his hand, to our teacher giving out entry tickets.

"En't 'avin' thirteen" one fat old boy declared, a podgy finger and thumb handing back the pale coloured ticket as he put his box down. Teacher's voice was soft but her eyes were turning steely.

"Now Bob, its the next one on the roll so there's nothing we can do about it. Take your ticket and go to the table on the right. Next, please." She sat back and adjusted her glasses.

"I'll 'ave twenty seven likes I 'ad last year," the old man's voice was obstinate, feet unmoving.

"Cum on Missus" shouted someone just outside the tent, "gie' 'im what 'ee wants and lets all get on wi' it."

Ma came along as things were quietening down, carrying a sponge cake filled with home-made strawberry jam and decorated with sieved icing sugar, it looked jolly nice on the glass stand that she stood it on, and the doily like a crisp frill round the bottom of it.

Three men and two ladies appeared.

Everyone was ordered outside, for the cards on their coats told us they were the judges; they were invited into the tent by 'Mr. Important' still with his trilby hat on, who held the tent flaps tightly behind them.

Mums and Dads slowly drifted back home but Liz and I stood watching the rest of the preparations. On a long stretch of new mown grass men were driving stakes into the ground and fixing ropes on them to keep the crowds out.

Beyond this, a pole several feet tall had been erected, and was being liberally brushed with cart grease by a chap called Charlie, red spotted hankie round his neck, cap on back to front and a pair of washed-out baggy trousers.

Women called to each other as they moved in and out of the tea tent carrying between them hampers of food and crockery, followed by an aproned woman cuddling a tea urn (that no one else was ever allowed to handle).

"Look at that cloud" she gloomed, "see it's ready to bust, but I bet it waits till Squire's Missus is givin' out prizes."

"Well keep thee 'ead down" laughed a stout woman dragging a couple of chairs across the grass, "and gi'e I a 'and wi' these tables."

Inside the tent the air was warming up, it smelt of crushed grass, clover and overheated bodies.

"Let's go and find out 'ow they judges be gettin' on" my friend suggested, my stomach squeezed a bit at her daring. "Not through the tent door" she hissed, pulling me down by my dress to the side of the tent, and in a second we lay flat on our stomachs.

All I saw as I lifted the loose bit between the tent-pegs was a feathered hat and the top half of a vase of sweet peas, and heard a woman's voice saying, "I think the blue ones are the best and really should have first prize."

"Oh I do 'ope they be our Mam's" whispered Liz in my ear, "for she's bankin' on gettin' that five bob to get I some new boots for school."

The sound of a cart brought us quickly to our feet, a pig was squealing its head off under a net on the back of it.

"That's the one they'll be bowlin' for" yelled the girl, as we rushed across to have a closer look at it.

The cart with its noisy occupant drew up next to the skittle alley, where several hurdles had been made into a rough pen.

Sid the driver got down, then his helper, a man with a small moustache blue striped apron, and boater.

They stood for a moment making their plans, Sid taking great puffs on his cigarette till the end glowed, a hand absentmindedly running grooves through his ginger hair, then both men came to an amicable decision.

"Thee 'old that net 'igh whilst I lets the tailboard down" said the helper going to the back of the cart. There wasn't a sound from inside as the pins were withdrawn, but as the board dropped a flash of pink and white then a large ball, as men and pig rolled on the ground.

"Take 'im off I" bellowed Sid's mate trying to scramble to his feet, his boater taking the full weight of the pig's trotter.

"Can't thee do nothin' right?" he wailed, as our pink friend raced with speed to the tea tent.

Women shrieked, hampers were dropped, cups spun out like tops in all directions, boys ran and so did we with the helper close behind flapping the net he'd torn off the cart.

"Mind my urn!" the aproned woman screamed as pig and children thundered past her.

"I'd giv' 'im a bright red shirt that I would if only I 'ad some boilin' water" she said.

In and out of the tent we ran, each one shouting instructions, till the poor beast made a wrong turn and was finally cornered in the hoopla stall.

There were squeals, howls of pain and "'old still you sod," as a bleeding hand held on to a hind leg, then Charlie was called, someone said the pig belonged to him and very soon had quieted the animal down then carried it out on his shoulder.

Women helpers laughed with relief as they picked up the broken cups and rubbed tea-cloths over the loaves of bread that hadn't too many trotter marks on them.

We reached the pen just as some food was being poured into the trough, and waited till the gulps and sloshy noises told us all was now fine.

"He damn well ought to eat" said Sid, climbing into the drivers seat, "arter all that runnin' about 'ee gi'e us."

"Can I 'ave a ride?" pleaded Liz looking at the lad, "remember we did gi'e yer a 'and to catch 'im." Sid agreed and held the horse steady by the reins as the girl heaved herself on to the seat alongside him.

The helper and I sat on the floor of the cart, dangling our legs over the edge against the tailboard, and had a bumpy ride along the rough track through the park past the village pump, stopping at the crossroads.

* * * * * *

At two o-clock Liz and I hurried to the park gate, Sunday best clothes on and carrying plimsoles (soft rubber shoes) for the races, my stomach tight with excitement and dinner that Ma had insisted on me finishing.

We joined Mums and Dads pushing babies in pushchairs and prams, bonneted and shawled old ladies in bathchairs, youths in plus-fours and open-necked shirts, cyclists, runners in white shorts and the village hob-nobs.

Behind the gate on the side which held the fete, one of the organisers sat with a small card table in front of him, and on it a tin box with a lock, roll of paper tickets, pipe, box of matches and a megaphone.

The man rose to his feet and looked at the watch fixed to a gold chain spread across his overhanging middle, then returned to his seat, sighed, counted his change and like all the rest of us waited.

The village fife and drum band now appeared, marching up the track to the strains of 'Colonel Bogey.'

"There's our Bill" shouted my friend, pointing to a tiny boy walking at the front of the band and striking a triangle. Like the rest of the bandsmen he was wearing his best clothes, and a pansy or forget-me-not pinned to the peak of his cap.

"Three cheers for Squire's widow" called out Parson in his Pulpit voice.

"She's bloomin' late" a woman beside me remarked; then followed smiles, bows and handshakes galore, as Widow, young Squire and his friends, honoured us with their presence.

The village Bobby, who earlier had leaned his bike against the hedge and locked the back wheel, now came forward and making a pathway through the crowd led them to the front.

Our chief guest stood smiling in her black silk dress edged with yards of filmy lace, till the clapping and cheers had almost died down, settled both feet firmly on the ground, placed gloved hands on the parasol and started the long speech to open the fete.

"Dear Friends," I heard, the voice faded into the distance as I started to read a large painted notice above the bobbing hat;

'Entry for Grown-Ups two pence,
Children one penny,
Babies in arms or pushchairs free if you show your ticket.'

My thoughts also dwelt on a bun, lemonade, and some ice-cream, with perhaps a few trys on the hoopla from the sixpence wrapped in a hankie in my pocket.

"...Now I declare this fete well and truly opened" a gloved hand gave a gentle push on the iron gate, and my dreams came to an abrupt end as someone gave an enormous shove from behind and Liz and I moved through faster than intended.

"Where's thee manners gals?" bellowed the policeman hauling us back and holding us firmly in place with an upraised arm.

"Let young Squire through — and his friends — Come along, Sir," he clicked his heels and gave a salute as they passed him — and the pay-box — without a word.

A long line followed slowly behind dropping pennies into the tin box and receiving a pale blue ticket with a number printed on it.

"Dun't lose thine" said my friend, tying hers in the top of her stocking, "yer might be lucky later on when they puts 'em in the hat for the draw."

We first called on the wild flower displays: six jars, still with jam labels on them but turned to the back, two cream-coloured earthenware jugs, and a very posh glass vase crammed with flowers and with the gold-edged FIRST PRIZE card on it.

"Dun't like that," Liz's voice showed her disappointment at not winning. "T'other village didn't ought to be allowed to compete wi' we, nor use they vases" she went on.

I was looking for mine and found it with a white card. "Highly commended but a pity tottle grasses were included."

We moved on down the row and saw knitted socks, ties, gloves, woolly hats with pom-poms, jumpers, shawls, tea-cosy covers, pram sets, mittens, bedsocks and knee warmers.

"Hey Liz, I bin lookin' for thee all over," a tall girl from our class called out, taking my friend by the arm and talking excitedly. "Yer knows that old nightie we all 'elped to put the lace and smockin' on? – well I'm damned if it 'en't got second prize."

Reaching the sewing table in just a few seconds after skirting a beehive and a display with cones of honey, we stood looking with astonishment at our handiwork. "Arter bloomin' Pelly tellin' us we wuz the wust workers in school! – just shows teachers dun't know what they be on about."

It took the three of us quite a time to see the leather work, paintings and drawings, wooden tables, trays, knife-boxes, and fretwork like golden embroidery.

Blinded with sunlight as we came out of the tent all I could see was a black blur, heard a megaphone call "Races at three thirty, there'll be good fun and rewards for each event, also don't forget there's a tea tent, plenty of stalls, and bowling for the pig to try your hand at."

"Dad's got fust prize for 'is beans," Liz's Mum told us, coming along with her latest addition that was squalling its head off for some nourishment.

"Now p'raps 'ee'l leave off moanin' — 'im and 'is bloomin' allotment," she bent over and rummaged amongst the baby's bedclothes, a soft pallid looking dummy was found, the woman popped it into her mouth to make it moist as the wails got louder.

"Shut thee row" we heard, as the warm wet globe was pushed into the tiny open mouth, there was a smothered sucking cry and then silence.

"E'nt thee racin'?" a couple of girls shouted, as they trotted past us, hair tied back, and wearing their plimsoles, and I noticed they were going towards the roped off part of the field, where a man standing on a box was swinging a rattle.

The crowd had gathered three deep behind the ropes. Mums were busy telling their offspring, "'Urry up and get all yer blinkin' things on."

Our Headmaster, wearing a stop-watch on a long tape round his neck, called his helper over and re-checked the programme.

Under the ropes Liz and I went as a megaphone blared out "Childrens race, one hundred yards" and we stood waiting one foot forward at the ready, till a shrill blast from the whistle was the signal to be gone.

Heart thumping, hair streaming out behind, I hardly felt my feet touch the soft mown grass. Cool, scented air brushed my cheeks and neck as I rushed towards the tape at the winning post.

Next came the egg and spoon race, followed by running in sacks, jumping over a pole, and dodging obstacles.

"I be glad that's all over with" said Liz and puffing like mad as we sat down on the ground and started changing from plimsoles to boots.

"Our Mam was dead keen I should try and win those five bobs, which'll go towards a coat or they boots for the winter."

From the fortune teller's tent opposite two young women appeared, one a blond wearing long ear rings and wobbling a bit on her high heeled shoes.

"Did yer 'ear what she telled I?" the blond asked her friend, and together they started giggling, "I'll 'ave two babies, a rich 'usband and a big 'ouse."

My friend waited till they'd passed us, leaving a strong scent of 'ashes of roses', then she burst out "That old fortune teller's a fake, everybody knows Rose has already got one that 'er Mam minds, and she'll 'ave another if she 'en't careful – well that's what our Dad said t'other night."

Races were over, the tea tent was crammed with folk, our aproned friend with her urn seemed to be having problems.

"I reckons this lot was made with one leaf" a youth told his girl friend, passing the cup along for her inspection.

"Or a couple of gnats" she replied poker faced, then they looked at each other and burst out laughing.

" 'Tain't tea that's weak 'tis thy bloomin' eyes" the woman retaliated fiercely, and as we left her lips were pressed in a thin line.

Lemonade in one hand and a bun in the other Liz and I watched two men sitting astride a pole and trying to knock each other off with a bag of flour. Both ended looking like ghosts as they fell on to the straw covered grass.

Headmaster checked his stop-watch and made an entry on his card.

"You've held out the longest so far" he informed them. "Anyone else?" he looked round for more volunteers.

All our strong men had disappeared to the end of the field, stripped to the waist and eager for a tug-of-war against the next village lads.

Wives and sweethearts took up sides, and we all cheered till we were hoarse with "Go on Sid, where's thee guts," and "Heave ho, boys."

The rope pulled first left till the men lay almost flat, then right as hobnailed boots bit deep into the soft turf.

Noise and the strong smell of sweat filled the air, then our team had a stroke of luck. Next village said " 'Twas done on purpose" when their end of the rope broke.

Squire's Widow gave out the prizes. Liz was in for a shock; there were no five bob pieces being handed over, only cake knives, beads, and a sewing basket for the girls, and when the boys lined up they got snake belts (elastic belts with a snake-shaped fastening) braces or collar studs.

The Major who ran the scouts made a short speech, thanking our Hostess for a "Lovely day in the park" and "How honoured and delighted we all were for her staying to give the prizes out," then he stood stiffly to attention as the fife and drum band played a 'new version' of 'God save the King.'

Jackdaws had already settled for the night in the church tower as we passed pushing wheelbarrow or truck, or carried baskets and things wrapped in newspaper.

"Didn't 'alf enjoy today" Liz told me as we walked slowly up the lane. "Wish there was summat else to look forrard to" she sighed. "Well there is" I reminded her. "Harvest Festival, Bonfire night, Xmas, and decorating the parish hall for the school party."

THIS WAS OUR VILLAGE

Chapter Eighteen

BE PREPARED

"Why en't you got yer uniform on?" a small girl asked me, she was holding the hand of her sister, a tall, thin, fair-haired Girl Guide who's smart dress and hat I very much admired.

"'Cos I'm still thinking about it" I lied, knowing full well that it was my mother's inability to find the half-crown that had stopped me from getting the uniform, and being enrolled.

Tonight, though, it would be different. I could feel the silver coin tucked for safety down the heel of my sock, and remembered the pleasure on Ma's face as she gave it to me.

My friend loosened her hand from the child's as the path came to an end. "Go straight 'ome our Dorothy" she told her, "and dun't thee stop muckin' about or the bogeys 'll get thee," came the warning.

The Girl Guide and I crossed the road and walked up the driveway to the 'Big House' between tall yew hedges still sprinkled with bright berries.

The chill wind struck us as we came from the shelter of the drive to a red-bricked yard surrounded by low buildings.

Outside the largest hung a row of lines held taut by wooden props, a few cloths fluttered lazily like pale grey flags near the open door.

"Be thee yer still, Aunt?" shouted Bess my friend, as we sloshed our way into the wash-house, trickles of water still running down the walls and making big puddles on the floor.

"I'm yer" came the answer, and through another doorway, busy ironing, stood a stout woman, sleeves rolled to the elbow, and a long very full white apron over her cotton dress, thick button boots, and heavy black stockings.

"Didn't walk on thee eyebrows I see" she observed in a cheerful voice, noticing the wet prints of our feet on the scrubbed floor, "Cum fer thee meetin' I suppose? Well thee'll 'ave to wait a bit till I've finished."

A large red hand held a maid's cap on to the ironing board whilst the other skillfully applied a goffering iron (crimping iron), two more were frilled as we stood watching; the woman humming gently to herself. As she worked, warm scented air from under the iron surrounded us. It was nearly dusk before she'd pressed the last one.

"Put the light on, Bess" requested Aunt, as the irons were stood on a brick shelf to cool off and the goffering tongs placed on a stand beside them. A soft glow filled the room as the woman moved to the airing cupboard, putting the newly ironed clothes in and taking a large checked coat, wide woollen scarf and brown felt hat out.

She took her time putting the garments on and my friend sat on the warm table swinging her legs as they exchanged news about their families.

More Guides wandered in. "Best be off now" remarked the woman, though she seemed reluctant to go. "Mind thee ties they knots right" was the last thing that we heard as she crossed the yard and out on to the driveway.

Three patrol leaders split us into groups.

"Now get they curtains up" we were

ordered, and each Guide collected one from an old laundry basket, and soon dens were made under the ironing table.

What activity there was, getting them straight and all the gear in, hanging the knotted cords on hooks and a picture of the Royal Family in a place of honour on the wall, then outside each curtained den we pinned the patrol badge: rose, robin, or violet.

Work finished and waiting for our leaders, boots were taken off and slides began along the smooth scrubbed tables, till a voice all stern, and very much in command called from the doorway.

"Guides to your places at once."

Red faced and feeling guilty we jumped to the floor and scrambled into some sort of a line in our stockinged feet, whilst a tall figure in blue uniform and highly polished black shoes

waited; what I noticed most about her was the
navy blue hat with a pleated cockade on one
side holding the brim up.

"Attention!" the vivid blue eyes looked
at mine for a second, then on all those wearing
uniforms who paraded in front of her, and she
wasn't satisfied until ties were neatened, belt
buckles brought dead centre on dresses well
pulled down over our knees.

"Those to be enrolled please step forward."

"Yes, Captain" three of us said meekly,
and standing in front of her, arms at the salute
I saw the motto 'Be prepared' over the doorway;
then with everyone watching, including our
Lieutenant who'd just walked in, we repeated
the solemn promise after Captain, and became
Girl Guides.

We were each given a badge, gold-coloured
and shaped like a clover leaf, the rest of the
evening was sheer magic; there was sending of

morse messages, exercises for posture, country dancing, followed by 'rich tea' biscuit eating, and mugs filled with lemonade.

The fun came to an end with prayers, the Catholics at one end of the room, we at the other, then standing in a large circle together sang the Guide's hymn to the tune of the 'Last Post.'

"Goodnight Girls" said our Captain, giving a salute which she was hoping we'd return, but most of us had already got as far as the wash-house.

"Come back here," Lieutenant's voice reached out stopping us dead in our tracks, we trailed back to find out what was going on.

"How would you like to go to camp in the summer?" we heard and stood there for a minute unbelieving, then everyone started to talk at once, till a patrol leader spoke for all of us,

"Please Miss, Captain I mean," she shuffled her feet a bit, "can we tell yer next week if we can come? 'cos if we gotta pay – well I dun't know what anybody else's Mam's like – but mine'll take 'er time makin' 'er mind up and findin' the money."

Next week was agreed and for a second time came the rush to the wash-house door. Bess and I waited till last for I'd been asked to collect my uniform. I took the half-crown from my sock, and saw it dropped into a tin box, the amount written into a notebook, then the precious brown paper parcel put into my eager arms.

Outside in the cold night air, Bess pulled me to a stop by my arm, "Do yer knows what yer bin and dun?" her face looked really serious, "only paid for all that stuff wi'out lookin' at it fust."

Down by the grey stone wall I tried the dress on, the hem rested on the top of my buttoned boots, cuffs caught the tips of my finger nails;

"Just right," my friend nodded, twirling me round, "arter all yer gotta allow for growin'" she went on, "and until then," she puffed the dress up and pulled the belt to its last hole, "well, thee'll just 'ave to put up wi' it bein' tight round yer middle."

Satisfied with her wisdom I took it off and re-wrapped the brown paper into a parcel, and for the rest of the walk home chatted about summer camp, next weeks tracking round Squire's wood, finishing with a camp fire supper that we'd cook with sausages and bacon.

THIS WAS OUR VILLAGE

Chapter Nineteen

CAMPING

"Get in line girls, please, for your last payment to the summer camp," ordered Captain, on one beautiful evening in late July, as she with our Lieutenant sat at a small table in the old laundry, with a money box and large red book in front of them.

"I bain't partin' wi' no more money" Bess informed me in a low voice, "not till I knows when she be takin' I."

A bright red patch appeared on our Leader's face at such impudence, as we slowly passed them and my money was handed in, it was checked twice then dropped into a grey canvas drawstring bag and the amount entered in the red book by her helper.

The evening passed with drill, games of tag, rounders, and a sing-song, but as soon as we could decently open our eyes and get off our knee from the evening prayer we scooted for the door to be first out.

"Elizabeth" a voice called out, my friend took her hand from the door knob and waited.

"Tell your mothers" Captain included us all but her blue eyes were paying full attention to Bess, "that I hope to take you to Douai Abbey for a week, sometime in August.

"We'll not be sleeping in tents as we're going camping for the first time, so the cricket pavilion has been kindly loaned to us and will be our Headquarters there."

"Hip, Hip," shouted Lieutenant, forcing a smile as she came forward, "Hooray" we bawled three times, waving hats above our heads and getting very excited.

"Fancy lettin' we lot among they old monks" I heard, as a pale-faced older girl came up to our group who were standing together talking. Her hat was perched at a saucy angle on her head, and her round button black eyes told you she missed nothing.

"Bet yer didn't know," her voice was very matter-of-fact, as she tightened her belt and pulled her dress up even higher "bet yer didn't know they old monks sleeps in cells, wears long brown cloaks wi' 'oods, and never stops singin'."

"Yer dun't 'arf tell 'em Lyddy, and 'ow do yer know all that?" she was challenged.

"'Cos our Bill, the one 'oo 'ad 'is chest bad and 'ad to go to sanatorium, was sent close to that place" said Lyddy, "sheep mindin', for 'is convalescence."

✶✶✶✶✶

August came and with it one special Saturday morning. We were all ready and gathered at the crossroads by the churchyard, impatiently waiting.

Mums and Dads hung about talking in groups, as babies crawled in and out amongst the kitbags.

"Dun't ferget, thee be goin' for a week's camp not a day or two" a harassed woman told her daughter, as once again all the clothes were taken out of the bag, laid on the grass, and recounted.

At last two blasts on a horn was heard, and down the street came a coal lorry.

"Come on Nick!" shouted a red-faced man, rushing up to the driver as he stopped close alongside. "Thee wants to keep away from they wenches at night" he bantered, "then 'praps thee'll be able to get up in the mornin'."

A lad, tall and thin, jumped from the driving seat, his good natured face wore a wide grin as he walked slowly round the back of the lorry, and let the tail-board down.

The inside had been swept out and washed down, the floor now covered in red coconut matting. A weather-proof hood had been fixed over the top, made of stiff black canvas and smelling heavily of tar.

"Cum on then, get in," Nick waved an arm towards us, we belted over as he hooked on a pair of steps. "And dun't forget, thee all sits on they forms at the side and leaves the short one lookin' on to the road for thee betters."

We climbed in pulling the kitbags behind us, stacking them into the darkest corner.

"Make way for this," our driver pushed on a laundry basket fastened with leather straps.

"Be that our grub for the week?" Lyddy asked, her hand resting on the top and longing to lift the lid. "Thee can 'ave a look if 'twill do thee any good" said Nick, then moved round the side of the lorry and started laughing.

You should have seen her face as she opened it up and discovered the basket was full to the brim, with broad beans.

"GOD love us, they bain't surely for we? there's 'nuff there for every pig in the village. Tell yer what," her face brightened, "when we gets safe in Abbey grounds we'll offer some to they old monks for their dinners."

"LYDDIA" the voice was stern. "Kindly close that basket and moderate your language."

"Yes, Captain," Lyddy saluted and sat down, our Leader and Lieutenant climbed aboard, and another hamper, marked groceries, was pushed on.

Up went the tailboard, fastened and tested by our driver, his grin gone and behaviour very respectful.

"We're now ready to start" came the order from inside.

"Yes, Mam," Nick touched the side of his face and ambled round to start the engine.

We drove through the village to cheers, shouted advice, and frantic waving, as the sun came from behind a cloud and beamed down on us. There was a beautiful smell of wet steam from the road, tarry hood, and peppermint sweets being eaten.

Halfway to camp Captain gave us permission to eat, a mountain of sandwiches in paper bags appeared as though by magic; cheese spread with piccalilli, bread and lard covered with brown sugar, sausages, pies and currant cake.

"Want a drop of this?" Bess held up

a large bottle of pale coloured liquid and
generously offered to pass it round.

"I hope that is not intoxicating" Captain
said sternly, my friend winced at her ignorance.
"Wun't make 'ee drunk if that's what thee
means, 'tis bee wine, and bloomin' delicious."

Leaving the main road behind, our way
led round twisty lanes that turned left and
right by the dozen, finally reaching a large
group of buildings with a high brick wall
surrounding them.

The lorry stopped. "Quick march" ordered
Captain almost before the last Guide had
clambered off, and in a single row we passed
through the main gate, Captain in front
leading, Lieutenant at the back to make sure
that we didn't forget our manners.

She needn't have worried for when we
reached the Abbey door and saw how grand it
was, every single one of us became tongue-tied.

"Welcome," called a grey-haired man, coming out from the porchway to greet us. He was tall and very upright, dressed in a long brown robe that reached to his ankles, and sandals that showed bare feet as he walked.

A silver cross hanging from a chain round his neck swung gently to and fro as he moved.

"Father" Captain beamed at him, "how good of you to allow us to camp in your grounds."

I didn't catch his answer, for Lyddy kicked my foot and pointed to a corner of the garden. There, sitting on a bench reading some books, were men, all dressed alike in flowing gowns.

"See, they be monks, like I told thee" she whispered.

We were taken to the chapel first, cool and dark with lovely stained windows, lines of polished pews, statues and pictures, the whole place filled with the scent of roses arranged in tall vases round the high altar.

Out in the hot sun again we blinked our eyes, and were given a tour of the garden, then the 'Father' shook our hands, said "Goodbye, and enjoy your week," and when he'd gone, as if by magic another monk appeared.

On the way to our Headquarters past two fields of fine mown grass, I was astonished to hear both Captain and Lieutenant call him "Brother," I noticed the hood fixed to his gown, then heard men's voices, singing in the distance. It was clear Lyddy hadn't been lying.

The first night seemed very strange, with all we Guides sleeping in one room.

"My bed scratches like bloomin' 'ell" Bess moaned, prodding the straw mattress, "'ere move up and let I try thine."

Boots were thrown at a girl who vowed

she'd tell Captain what was going on, one hit the target, giving her a beautiful black eye and she howled like mad, till somebody got up, and gave her a packet of sweets from their knicker pocket.

Captain came in later and shone her torch round, "Goodnight girls," nobody bothered to answer, so she took the opportunity to open every window and returned to her private room on the balcony above us.

Bess and I sat for a long time after that, looking out on fields that stretched way into the distance, watched the moon come out, the monks fade into the shadow of the buildings and smelt the sweet scent of budlea on the night air.

What a marvellous time we had, with walks and an excursion to Windsor Castle, looking at Queen Mary's Dolls House, lots of stairs with no carpets, and models of knights in armour.

We saluted a sentry who Bess said must be "dead and just stuffed?" 'cos he didn't move, not even when we kicked his foot.

I bought a stick of rock for my brother and sister, a crest china cat with painted whiskers for Ma, and a match box holder that Lieutenant said was a "real bargain" for two-pence and would please Dad, then found I had four pence left to see the week through.

Two days before we left, our folks came to visit us, but I was too busy cleaning the pots and billycans, so whilst Ma chatted and walked around Bess and I took the opportunity to dig a big pit and bury the rest of the broad beans.

That evening, and the next we had carrots and peas for supper, home-grown tomatoes and some beautiful lettuces, and tried not to show our guilt when Captain remarked that "she just couldn't think what rubbish we'd found to have to dig a new pit that afternoon."

On the last day it rained hard, so the invitation to use the 'gym' was quickly accepted, and soon we were standing in a long line ready to jump over a wooden thing called a 'horse.' We jumped, missed and fell onto coconut matting, got up and tried all over again.

Next came skipping, rope ladders were scaled, and a medicine ball hurled, and when that was finished, one of the monks came in and gave Lieutenant a large tin of biscuits to share amongst us.

Nick came early the next morning with the coal lorry to fetch us, kitbags and two empty hampers were hauled on first, and whilst he waited sitting in the cab, reading his paper and smoking a Woodbine, we marched to the Abbey to say our goodbyes.

"Thank you, Father, for making our stay such a splendid one," Captain was bursting with gratitude, then each Guide went up and shook hands with him, and after he'd blessed us we departed.

As we rode homewards Captain asked "Well, what have you all enjoyed most during the week?" "Windsor Castle" some said, "Gym and biscuits," "Mam comin," "They monks" said Lyddy and got smartly rebuked.

"And you?" the blue eyes looked into mine, "Everything" I promptly replied and she seemed satisfied.

How could I tell her that I'd always remember the monks singing in the chapel, the scent of budlea and the moon carpeting the dew-soaked lawn.

THIS WAS OUR VILLAGE

Chapter Twenty

THE TREAT

Summer holidays were slowly coming to an end, but today there was one more event we'd been looking forward to; the school treat held every year on the Downs above the village.

"Our Dad sez yer can sit on the waggon in front we us," Liz promised, as we walked across to the rick-yard, each carrying a spoon, tin mug and plate, and stopping at the gate watched her father and a youth thoroughly brushing down two large cart-horses ready for the waggon that would take us to the outing.

The animals showed no signs of irritation at the extra grooming, food bags on and slowly munching, as hooves were wiped with an oily rag and the long hairs on each leg combed till they looked like white silk gaiters.

Soon the brushes were tossed to one side and the plaiting began; first the mane, red and yellow braids entwined as each section was twisted, finally the tail, plaited to a thick polished sausage shape, the end turned under and held fast with a wide yellow and red bow.

The carter's helper went into the stable close by, returning a few minutes later with some of the harness. Sunlight gleamed on leather and brasses, as each piece was placed on and securely fastened.

Both workers stood back when they'd finished, and viewed their charges, seemed well pleased with what they saw and removed the nosebags, then led the animals over to the waggon, brightly painted and standing under an old elm tree.

"Shuv 'in back, Boy," shouted the exasperated carter to the lad, as several attempts were made to get the unwilling beast between the shafts, and accomplished only after much clomping of hooves, head tossing, and swearing from the two men.

The lead horse was then brought into position, the trace fixed and all was ready for moving off.

"Come you lot, hop on smartish" Liz's Dad called out to us, and we who had waited so long for this moment rushed over.

"Mind thee dun't break thee blasted legs" came the warning, as we tried to climb on to the hub of the wheel, slipped and had to be hoisted up by a strong arm.

A long thin whip was handed to the

carter by his helper, who was once again told in great detail all the jobs he had to do, ending with "And dun't thee ferget to close the stable door properly afore thee leaves, else we'll 'ave all they chickens roostin' inside."

Satisfied that his orders had been heard the carter tightened the reins, we heard "Gee up" and clicking noises several times, the horses moved forward at a steady old pace, pulling the waggon through the yard to the crossroads.

A second waggon stood waiting when we arrived, already filled to overflowing with older children, who squirmed and shoved, shouted and cried till steps were brought and teachers climbed on to quieten them and the helpers.

We took on board the tea-urn lady who was one of our helpers, dressed all in black and hugging a big black kettle. Two large enamel teapots were pushed on, baskets with loaves of bread, a seven pound jam pot labelled 'apple and plum,' mysterious things rolled in a white cloth and two churns of water.

Four ladies in flowing overalls and bare arms pushed their way through the crowd, settling themselves and their babies on the floor of the waggon. Infant pupils, some holding flags, got squeezed in between them, then at the very last minute someone remembered the trestle table and piled it on despite loud protestings from all sides.

Mugs were waved, and enamel plates used as drums, with spoons banging out rhythms against them, and Mums watched with small children clinging to their skirts, as both waggons crawled slowly out of the village and up the steep hill.

Once out in the open the sun gave us his full attention, and dust from the road thickly covered everything. How I longed for a drink but knew that a long wait was in front of me so closed my eyes, and listened to the horses hooves, jingling harness, voices and bursts of laughter.

As the last farm was passed the chalk road petered out, leaving only a stony track for the final climb.

"Jump out all you lads, and lighten the load for they 'osses" said the carter, and teachers, women and older pupils pushed the waggons from behind until we reached the top, on the Ridgeway.

Scents of warm grass, moon-daises, and red clover filled the air, peewits called and hedge sparrows quarrelled; and along the Ridgeway, as far as the eye could see, the trees shimmered in the hot afternoon sun.

Horses and carts were drawn into the shade of a clump of beeches nearby, and great activity started on making a wood fire, and cutting sandwiches.

The women in overalls got the trestle up, after a lot of arguing whether it should stand near the hedge and catch the flies, or out in the open and melt the margarine.

Teachers stood in a group admiring the view, everyone seemed busy except us, then a thin boy, hands in trouser pockets, suggested we "go and try findin' "old King" who's s'posed to be buried yer."

The "King's" grave was a mound several feet high, and covered with grass and small trees.

"Must 'ave bin yer for a bloomin' long time" said Liz, climbing to the top and padding around. "What about diggin' in it?" suggested the boy, drawing his jack knife out of his pocket and plunging the blade into one or two places.

"P'raps we'll find 'is skull or some treasure" one of our friends said, as we moved round the side of the mound where we wouldn't be seen.

A couple of bottles, jaw of a rabbit, and a dead rat had been found when the bell from a distance told us tea was ready, and we girls all dashed off to be first at the table leaving the boys to find some dock leaves to wipe their hands and the knife blade on.

We had jam or paste sandwiches, and curranty buns, mugs of tea strong enough to dye your hair in and heaped with sugar, a dash of milk and a powerful taste of wood smoke.

Then Parson, who'd just arrived, made us all stand and give thanks to the Almighty for what we'd had and with my eyes closed and standing quite still, I could hear the leaves on the trees moving gently to and fro.

"Fetch the sacks, Boy," came the command from Headmaster, "and you, Girl, get the egg and spoon box," then a flat spot on the Ridgeway was found shortly after that and races were run by each class.

Parson's wife gave out the prizes.

"Fancy thee winnin' that," Liz's eyes lingered on the pencil box in my hand, "will yer swap it fer this?" she held up a necklace of green beads, "Bain't my colour anyway — and green allus brings I bad luck."

We exchanged prizes as Headmaster called for us all to come and make a circle, he thanked Parson and Parson's wife, teachers, helpers and the carters, even the horses got a mention till we got sick and tired of hearing his voice and wondered how much longer we'd have to stand to attention.

The sun, brilliant red from it's efforts was slowly moving down to reach the hills,

as baskets and trestle table got stacked into
the waggons, then the tea-urn helper and
her kettle, teapot and the milk churns were
pushed on, followed by the overalled ladies and
their babies.

We heard "Steady boys" and "Whoa" as
waggons vanished down the steep track, with
the drogues on, and all who'd been asked to get
off the waggons downhill took a short cut to
the bottom of the field, caught up with the
waggons and were helped back on.

Liz's Dad let me sit with them as he'd
promised and let me hold the horses reins in his
strong hands.

"Go on Snowball get a move on" I shouted
very excited. " 'Tain't no good bawlin' at 'in"
I heard from behind, "let's tickle 'in wi' this,"
the man loosened one hand and gently flicked
his whip on the horse's nose.

Mugs and prizes were flourished to
waiting Mums at the crossroads, as waggons

came to a halt and down poured the children, all talking and shouting at once.

Then our Teacher called out "Three cheers for Headmaster."

"And a lovely day" said a sunburnt lady, covering her bright red arms with her overall.

My friend and I sat alone on the waggon, whilst Snowball and Ginger pulled us back to the rick-yard, and as we sat waiting for her Dad to finish work we looked again at the prizes we'd exchanged.

"I dun' 'arf like this," Liz opened the pencil box and carefully lifted out the tray. "See, our Mam'll be able to put 'er crocher 'ooks on top and underneath all they knittin' needles."

She must have seen my surprise as she closed the lid and rubbed a grubby hand along the polished top. "See, I be keepin' this to gi'e our Mam on 'er birthday," she explained, "'cos

I 'ent got no money to buy 'er a present."

We left the waggon and crossed the yard, each holding a bunch of wild flowers for our mothers, stopping at the stable door to say goodnight to Snowball and Ginger, who tossed their heads as they heard our voices and took the sugar lumps with tongues like velvet.

"Nice to be 'ome, en' it?" the girl spoke softly as she stroked the horses heads and seemed in no hurry to be gone, and when we finally moved, a cool breeze had blown up and the last of the day faded into night clouds.

THIS WAS OUR VILLAGE

Chapter Twenty-One

MARKET DAY

"Can we borrow one of your gals today?" called out a woman (whom I recognised as Emily) coming up the garden path where my mother was busy planting out pinks and big daises.

She was dressed in a smart fawn tweed coat reaching nearly to her feet, the collar like a long scarf tossed over one shoulder. One hand strayed to her ginger curls refusing to stay put under the flat broad brimmed hat trimmed with two large red cotton roses.

She came closer and I noticed she was

carrying a fat piglet of a baby, red-faced and bonneted in green, who still drowsy with sleep was about to protest at being snatched from the pram but his mother got there first and press-studded a dummy into the puckered up mouth.

"We'em going to market today" she explained to us, "and I wants someone to mind our Perce while I'ops round for the bargains."

The baby heard its name, looked up and gave two sucks on its dummy, closed its eyes and sank back again into sleep.

I at once volunteered and was told to go upstairs and tidy my hair, change my knickers and put on my best dress and boots.

I could hear them laughing and talking in the kitchen below. "Yes the day was right for the four miles easy walking," then the sound of the lid on the bread crock being replaced as Emily's voice once again repeated

"Dun't thee worry about eatin' we got plenty of victuals for a nice little stop on the way."

Ma saw the three of us to the top of the lane then waved and smiled as we turned the corner, she'd be going back to her garden and the flowers she loved with not a soul in the place to hinder her.

Halfway up the village the rest of the party had gathered, "Wondered where you'd got to" said a gypsy-looking woman attired in bright blue. "En't got all day to 'ang about" she protested to no one in particular, hands and feet betraying her impatience to be gone.

The sun shone, though a cool breeze reminded us that it was early autumn.

We were sorted out and started walking as the church clock struck nine. Mums led the way pushing prams that looked like miniature trucks, loaded with coats, babies and food; toddlers hanging on to the women's skirts or anything else they could grasp or hold. Boys in Norfolk jackets and breeches followed, others in jerseys, long black stockings and outsize caps, small girls in pigtails; and keeping an eye on things like sheepdogs on duty, ambled we older girls right at the back.

Not that anyone was in a hurry to get through the village, there was too much to be seen and talked about.

First a halt at the old barn to read the notices and pass our opinion; 'RUMMAGE SALE for Catholic church funds'; 'WHIST DRIVES every Wednesday'; 'Jars please for next JAM SESSION' (that one over a month old), with a smaller note and a new date that had been fixed to it later, signed by the secretary and reading "Please will you bring MORE JARS this time."

"Allus wantin' summatt she be," came

from the reader behind me and all decided to move on.

Past the inn we went and down the hill, between the high banks covered with dead grass, unripe blackberries, nettles and toadstools.

Overhead stretched an archway of elms, their long branches like witches arms moving slightly in the breeze. All around wetness and rotting smells, I shuddered and suddenly felt scared and moved closer to Emily and her friends.

Soon we came out into the sunshine again to the bridge on the turnpike road, stopping for a while to watch the coots and moorhens near the stream and round the rushes.

The boys tired of that quickly and climbed the uneven wall, making wobbling attempts to reach the end before they fell off, mothers shouted at such daring and toddlers cried, they were picked up and bundled on to the ends of prams, given biscuits and pacified.

Threats of "Tell thee father" and "bein' skinned alive" finally got them down and they trailed behind sullen and resentful, arguing amongst themselves who should carry the scout pole they'd brought along.

"Gi'e it yer" said one woman at last as it was snatched from the boy's grasp and tied with a bit of string on to the pram handle.

About halfway we stopped for a chat to a man called by his relatives 'Uncle Billy', who in shirt sleeves and rust-coloured trousers sat by the roadside. There was a lull in the conversation, then "She be goin' to be widened" he told us, looking down the old road we'd just travelled on, "'tis they blasted cars breakin' 'er up too," and he clenched his fist when we told him that we had four cars in the village already. "Osses and carts is all we wants, wench" he turned to me, "Osses and carts."

"Ee's nuts" said his niece amiably as she passed with her companion, "anybody as can't keep up with the times must be, stands to reason."

Her friend made no reply, for the others had stopped to rest and eat. I wondered what the dinner would be, as babies were hauled out of prams and laid on bits of blanket by the hedge, for last time on an outing we'd had chitterlings in lumps of bread followed by 'Salisbury beer' – brown, gingery and delicious.

The boys hovered around and were told to "Sit down and bide quiet."

Emily, I noticed, was the last to unload.

I saw onions, lumps of cheese and slices of pickled pork, drawn from sugar bags and pieces of muslin, it was all placed on a clean flour bag on top of a hastily raised pram hood.

"Are you all ready now" shouted Emily

as she lifted up the baby's mattress and pulled out a large bundle wrapped in newspapers and tied with string; it was quickly unfastened and out fell baked potatoes in their jackets, everyone helped themselves and returned to their places by the hedge to enjoy them.

Babies were held and fed, those that could sit up or crawl joined us, they were given the same food as we had only it was chopped up with a small sharp knife.

One baby was given a carrot which it sucked and nibbled in turn, whilst its mother, seeing all was quiet started handing round the lemonade. I leaned back against a small tree and closed my eyes wishing with all my might that Ma had come, how could she give up such a lovely treat, the company and the fun.

Suddenly there was a cry that the carrot-sucking baby had disappeared, and right beside my feet, out of the ground it seemed, a muffled howling could be heard.

"Ee's in the drain" shouted a boy on the other side of the hedge. "I can see 'im from this end." We all raced to where the lad was standing, bumping heads as we bent to look. "Little sod" the mother said with feeling, vainly attempting to pull her infant out.

"Let's fetch the policeman" suggested Emily. "What! three miles?" retorted the policeman's wife, "'sides he'll be eatin' 'is dinner" she went on indignantly.

No one spoke for everybody was thinking hard, then the boys remembered the scout pole; in a trice it was untied from the pram and placed into position and with a small cushion to soften the blow given a mighty push up the drain pipe.

How we laughed when the baby shot out the other end, intact and roaring its head off, it was picked up, cried over, wiped heartily and returned to the pram.

A few moments later we were ready, with our goods stowed away and back on the road heading for town.

It was one o-clock when we reached the market, now in full swing, and pulled into a side street just off the market square. The women straightened up the babies, gave them a kiss, gathered the shopping bags and gave us our instructions.

"Dun't thee talk to strange men or let they give yer presents. Keep in the square and no goin' down they alleys." This with other bits of advice thrown at us as they crossed the road and were soon lost amongst the crowds.

"Well come on, I ben't 'angin' about yer for two hours" said Pat, the eldest, as we stood huddled in a group not knowing quite what to do. "I votes we wheels this lot up and down for a bit and 'as a look at things, starting with old Alfred."

"What a bloomin' cheek!" Pat stopped her pram, and we saw propped against the statue of a very noble man, an old rusty bike.

"Ee was our King you know, Saxon" the girl continued, going close and patting the stone with pride. She wheeled the bike away whilst I waited and for the first time I saw the stone figure, his face turned forever in the direction of his birthplace, robed and crowned, a scroll held tightly in his left hand, in the right hand a mighty battleaxe.

Pat returned and we noticed a man working on the stall close by, he wore a straw boater perched on the back of his head, striped blue and white apron tied round his waist with wide tape, and was busily arranging fish in neat designs on the table. In front of him mackerel, herrings, dabs, kippers and bloaters, sprats, bowls of shrimps and winkles by the plateful, cods heads and fins on a big dish.

Price tickets lay in piles on one side, together with a chopping block, two thin knives, a pair of scales and a variety of old newspapers.

I stood watching with amazement as fish were weighed, chopped in half and deprived of head and tail, the man wiping the knives, scales and his bald head every few minutes, with a cloth that was tucked into the top of his apron.

There were stalls with rows of rabbits, chicken and raw red meat, breaded hams and basins of brawn.

Everywhere movement, the smell of fish, oranges and meat, saturating our clothes and hair in the warm afternoon sun.

A man stopped us, around his neck a strap holding a tray of matches, "Only a penny a box" he said, moving his crutches a little in an effort to balance on one leg. His companion, completely blind, and wearing a row of medals played the violin till my heart ached. Ma had talked about these First World War soldiers and how little was done for them.

Pat bought a sherbert dab with a Union Jack on top, which we both licked in turn as we moved around, our sight-seeing coming to an abrupt halt by a large crowd of people in front of us.

"Walk up, walk up," shouted a huge man in navy blue. "This sight you'll never see again" we were told, "for before you stands the modern Houdini." He pointed to a thin, balding and wrinkled figure beside him.

"Must be all of eighty" Pat whispered, half to herself as we used the prams to get a good view at the front by the cobbles.

"I am now about to put this 'ere man in a canvas jacket," the huge man went on, "fasten it like this," he whirled his victim round so that everyone saw the straps. "Now the bottom of his jacket will be tied to his legs with chains." These were given such a mighty tug that the trussed up man was lifted off the ground; "and we'll tie his arms," the voice triumphant.

I felt a throbbing feeling start up in my neck as the canvas-covered arms were tied firmly behind him and the man was exhibited again, the huge man drawing a gold watch out of his pocket and counting down the seconds.

"Three—Two—One" he shouted, the wrinkled old chap fell to the ground, wrestled this way and that way then wriggled and squirmed like an eel.

"Help him you fool" Pat shouted to the huge man as chains clanked on the cobbled stones and excitement ran through the crowd.

There was no need for assistance; the tied up man quickly untangled himself, red faced and sweating hard he stood and bowed to us all, then he picked up a hat and passed it round with great speed before we moved on to other interests, and half an hour later whilst waiting in a side street, over everything else that was going on could be heard the huge man's shouting "walk up, walk up, walk up."

Just on three o-clock, chattering and laughing the women returned, loaded down with goods which were hastily stuffed in baskets down the sides of prams, behind pillows and under mattresses; toddlers were lifted up on to the remaining space and we waited for two boys to join us.

"Ripe bananas," called a man from the other side of the road, "only a shilling a bunch." The voice seemed familiar and very refined, the women at once recognised him, collected some money between themselves and sent one of the older girls over to buy the lot.

The boys having now turned up we started on the four mile trek for home, leaving the men packing their stalls and the paths littered with newspapers, fish heads and rotting fruit.

Everyone talked about the bargains they'd bought as we trudged back along the turnpike, stopping every now and then to take one toddler off the pram and lift another on to it.

Boys hung behind to look at tops and bags of marbles they'd purchased, the gypsy woman was impatient at our progress.

"Come on Missus get a move on" she bawled
out to the policeman's wife busy sharing a
banana with her friend, then on remembering
who they'd bought it from, lowered her voice
and sounded very serious.

"Did yer notice who sold us they?" she
asked. "Course we did" the women answered.
"Fancy 'im gettin' four months hard labour
for a bloomin' forty pounds" they said. "And
I bet he pinched it for his swanky old woman
to get a new dress though God knows what for"
Emily joined in.

The policeman's wife suddenly realised
we were listening and told us the wickedness
of stealing however much we felt tempted, the
lecture lasting till a stop came to finish the
doughnuts and lemonade.

In no time the bridge was reached, we
turned off the turnpike and walked the dark
road to the village, my thoughts not with

the overhanging elms, dead plants, or even my friends. I was thinking of the banana man and the fourpence I'd so recklessly given him. Would Ma consider helping someone, "an emergency," for that's what she'd said when she handed the money to me.

We passed the inn with the funny sign outside and walked on to the crossroads by the church, parcels were handed over and promises made for another trip together.

Emily thanked me for coming and told me to "'ang on a minute." Drawing out a newspaper full of herrings from under the sleeping baby, she chose a nice fat one and shoved it in a used sugar bag.

"That's for your tea" she told me, handing over the present, "just a nice little 'thank you', dear, from Perce yer and me."

THIS WAS OUR VILLAGE

Chapter Twenty-Two

HORSES FOR EVER

I was on the way to the big shop in the village to spend my weekly pocket money – a halfpenny – putting my hand every now and then into the large pocket of my dress to feel if it was still there.

Rosie, my friend, walked a few paces in front, balancing first on one foot, then the other as we reached the narrow earth bank above the road. Her dark hair which reached to her waist was held in place with a large brown slide shaped like a butterfly, tiny glass beads shining on each wing, and over her old-fashioned dress the laciest pinafore you ever saw.

"I've got twopence to spend," she called out, turning round carefully and holding up the coins. I wasn't jealous, she hadn't a mother and used to come and share mine when she felt lonely, or if her Granny was busy.

We waited whilst some stable lads and several racehorses came slowly along the road; the long legs and sleek bodies of the animals quivering with anxiety, eyes wide open and fearful, steps dainty but faltering.

Some of the lads walked beside them holding the animals firmly with short reins, others rode on the backs of their charges, knees pressed against the protecting blanket held by the saddle.

The front horse swayed as it reached us, seeing for the first time the flutter of Rosie's pinafore. "Keep still you two can't you?" the man called out angrily, trying to calm the beast as it danced in our direction.

"We haven't moved yet" we bawled back fed up with waiting, our voices now almost level with the animal's ear; up went the front legs immediately and a fine old tussle broke out between horse and man.

There was bank scrambling, rein pulling, and language such as you'd never heard before, till finally, with foam shining along its body and trembling violently the animal gave in, dropping back on to the firm road. Those horses and men who'd waited behind now moved on, as we stood holding each other's hands, well out of danger.

"My Dad says they didn't ought to be allowed near people," Rosie's voice sounded a bit unsteady. "And my Dad" I told her "says men are a cruel lot of devils anyway, making them run like that for money," but the incident was soon forgotten as we crossed over the road to the big shop.

It was a grand looking place outside, all timber and red bricks, with fancy chimneys. We'd been told at school that the house was Tudor and that some rich woollen-merchant must have lived there years ago.

A small extension, newly painted and attached to the side of the building, stood where the old shed used to be, covering the spot where the last shop-owner had drowned himself in a large storage tank of paraffin.

"Do you think that poor man suffered long?" Rosie asked, as we stood looking at all the good things on show in the window, gathering some of the wet paint on to our clothes, as we pressed closer to see more.

The door beside us opened and an elderly woman came out carrying an old sack filled with food, slung it across her back and trudged off up the road to the Downs, leaving the door wide open and showing a room crammed with customers waiting to be served; some craning their necks to see the bacon on display or helping themselves to cheese tasters, others having a good old gossip as the owner of the shop, a short, thin looking man with a trilby hat perched on the back of his head and pencil behind his ear, darted in and out of the back door with boxes of food, later to be delivered in the village.

His wife was a tall thin woman with red-gold hair piled high in coils around her head, and long gold earrings dancing like ballerinas as she stooped and straightened at her work.

"Thank you very much" we heard, over and over again, as she tossed coins and silver into the half-opened drawer, or fixed the pound note on the clip. "Much obliged I'm sure," the voice and her smile put on every morning with her overall.

There was going to be time for a jolly good look round so we started with the glass-topped counter showing a long row of Carrs chocolate biscuits, oval and square shapes, plain or milky, each in its own paper.

There were pale sugary biscuits in neat lines, inside a cream-coloured tin partly hidden by the lid, with 'Pat-a-Cake' written along the top and a painting of a very fat baby in the centre, arms outstretched and mouth open in a toothless smile. Cadbury's chocolates at sixpence a quarter (which as far as I was concerned would stay there for many a long day), and open boxes of liquorice allsorts.

There were figs, and peaches in fancy glass jars, treacle which you could buy by the pint from a small barrel with a saucer catching the drips from the leaky tap, rows of spice drawers, and a marble wash-stand, the top covered with all sorts of cakes.

Over our heads, (and only just, in some places), hanging on hooks was an assortment of tin ware: kettles, frying pans and teapots, small baths and buckets, irons, paraffin stoves, watering cans, string and garden tools; in fact there was so much hanging from the ceiling that it was nothing short of a miracle no accident had occurred.

Nothing was priced so guessing games and arguments abounded, adding to all the other noises in the shop.

Rosie and I having looked at all the sweets on display, counted how many we'd get for our money and with a long wait ahead pushed our way to the new extension.

A glass cabinet held reels of ribbons – pale blue, green, and brown; pink satin with delicate edging; stiff black and grey elastic.

All the drawers at the bottom of the

cabinet were open, some wider than others and a confusion of underwear hung from them nearly to the floor.

White calico bodices trimmed with coarse lace, winter combinations of all sizes, black stockings, woollen scarves, and ladies bloomers; gloves, babies bibs, and handkerchiefs kept company with slides, hairbrushes and combs in the last drawer,

At the side of the counter stood a life-sized cardboard figure of a lady dressed in the latest afternoon black dress for maids, complete with coffee coloured cap, apron and cuffs, looking with disdain and lasting displeasure at all the muddle round us.

We sat down on the two cane chairs close to the cabinet for a rest, leaned back and surveyed the ceiling, and I noticed suspended from it on a fine silken rope, a lovely pair of slippers, red, with gold linings and pom-poms.

If only I could have those I thought, then

noticed my friend was looking at them too, and knowing her granny gave her everything she asked for decided I'd have to make her forget them.

"Bet you're afraid to try those on" I challenged her, looking around the shop first to see if anyone was watching us. It worked, Rosie took her gaze from the slippers and was soon clomping up and down in a new pair of hobnailed boots.

The next to be sampled were grey buttoned shoes with high heels, then carpet slippers and hard shiny gaiters, leather belts ... and hats were the last on the list when there came two sharp raps on the shop door.

The hats were taken off. Everyone stopped talking and turned to look. The shopkeeper said something to his wife in a low voice, scowled, his eyebrows jumping up and down with vexation. She opened the division by the counter and crossed to the shop door, lifting the latch and letting a blast of cold air in.

A horse's head pushed its way into the shop, its tongue dripping with moisture, a pair of soft brown eyes viewed us with some surprise which we returned at such a strange customer.

On the animal's back sat an important-looking young woman in riding breeches and tight coat, her hair covered with a smart felt hat, the riding crop used as a knocker still in her hand.

"Yes Miss?" the shopkeeper's wife bowed slightly, voice respectful. "What can I do for you, Miss?". She stood waiting for the order, with the palm of one hand nervously stroking the back of the other.

"Our dog biscuits and meal didn't come with the rest of the delivery, could you get them to the house before lunchtime."

Before anyone could reply the horses head

had disappeared, pulled in the direction of the park by a strong tugging of reins; there was a mere brushing of riding crop on the horse's flanks and a movement of knees pressed into its body as rider and animal departed.

"Certainly Miss, much obliged I'm sure Miss" called the harassed woman to thin air, closing the door and coming back to the counter, her hands still making stroking motions as she smiled apologetically at the customer who's order had so rudely been interrupted.

"Wasn't I fust?" said that person with some show of temper. "You were" came the exasperated answer from trilby hat and fast moving eyebrows.

"Well then – why wasn't she kept waitin' that's what I wants to know," a grubby hand pointed to the window and fast disappearing rider.

"'Cos you knows who she is" came a voice

from the back of the shop, "and they're busy getting ready for the fox hunt."

It was the shopkeeper's son who gave out the news, a tall lad with glasses and bags of cheek.

"How do thee know?" argued the belligerent customer. "'Cos I've just delivered a ton of stuff there." He saw the look on his father's face, and the conversation came to an abrupt end.

"Well I 'ope she bloomin' falls off" thundered our furious friend, and still angry at the slight she'd received tossed what money she owed on to the counter and started packing her basket.

"Much obliged, I'm sure" the tone was soft, grateful, and very humble. "Well I en't" was the retort as the woman flounced out closing the door with a mighty bang, leaving only the sound of coins being dropped into the open till.

Order returned as father and son left the

shop to make deliveries; we were the next in the line to get some service, and chose a couple of bars of Sharps creamy toffee wrapped in waxed paper with blue edging and with the picture of a man wearing a bowler hat, monocle, and with a parrot sitting on his shoulder.

With our money handed over we rushed to the door, ignoring the pleas to "Come again and bring your custom" and if she was "Much obliged" it fell on deaf ears for we were off to the 'Big House' to see the start of the fox hunting.

* * * * * *

Lots more people had decided to take a look. The grassy patches leading up the drive were crowded with women and children, a smaller band of men, some leaning on bikes, watched from the road.

In front of the house on the gravel surrounding a circle of green stood groups of horses and grooms, the latter standing patiently holding the animals steady by a short rein, whilst their owners looking very much at ease in the saddle held loud conversations with their friends.

All were dressed in tightly fitting red jackets, white breeches, and black peaked, caps, carried riding crops, and wore long highly polished black boots.

My father remarked to a man standing beside him, that "Plenty of hard work by some poor bloke had gone into all that get-up" and a lengthy conversation followed ending with both men picking "the riders" from "the duffers" by the way they sat on their horses.

We were pushed on to the grass as two young women rushed up with some speed, sitting astride their horses like men and wearing almost the same type of clothing.

They were greeted with low whistles

from youths lounging by the roadside, and cold glances from old fashioned Mamas who were turned out in full hunting gear, hats polished and skirts hung in long careful folds, showing just a hint of boots as they sat side-saddle on their horses. All wore snowy cravats round their necks, fixed in place with a small jewelled brooch.

Horses whinnied, men shouted, ladies laughed heartily, and the crowd looked on; clearly they were waiting for someone.

She came, the haughty young rider who'd knocked on the shop door with her riding crop this morning, but surrounded now by dozens of hounds, pouring, so it seemed, from everywhere.

She called them to "heel" in the same voice that she had used to the shopkeeper's wife and they responded immediately.

Squire appeared dressed in a red fitting coat and white breeches, his head snugly encased in a black velvet riding cap with a button on the top.

As Master of the Hounds his horse was waiting in front of the others, he was helped on and after a few words to the groom put his lips to the horn as though to try it out.

Cheers went up as the front door of the house was opened by a shabbily dressed servant holding a silver tray covered in glasses filled with sparkling liquid. Each rider was handed one, held it high and shouted "To the hunt."

"Here, Here" replied the elderly hunting man at the back, who by the look of his clothes one would have thought he never got down from his horse.

"That's old Reggie" whispered the boy to his friend, "ee's the one as drops the pennies for we to pick up." "And the tanners" (sixpenny pieces) interrupted someone else, pushing as near to the riders as he dared.

'Reggie,' his drink now finished, slumped

into the saddle as if to take a nap, eyes closed and head drooping nearly on to his chest. The boys stared at him anxiously willing him awake, as horses pawed the ground and grooms gave the final check round.

All was now ready, Squire gave the signal to move off, Reggie came to life, up went his arm and a shower of pennies and silver coins fell to the ground. Boys scrambled for money, risking the horses hooves, as the hunters with their riders moved slowly down the drive and through the village to some fields close to the Downs.

We tailed on behind them for a good mile before turning back, hearing now and again on the breeze blasts from the horn, and the excited baying of hounds.

THIS WAS OUR VILLAGE

Chapter Twenty-Three

AUTUMN FRUITS AND SPELLS

"How do you spell chutney?" I asked my sister as we sat at the kitchen table one sunny afternoon, in front of us a packet of transparent jam-pot covers, a pencil and a long strip of labels.

Ma called the word out letter by letter as she stood stirring the contents of a large black saucepan on the open stove. Then, deciding it was ready, wound a cloth round the handle to protect her hands and carried it over.

The thick wad of newspapers close to us dried to a crisp on top, as hot saucepan came down heavily on them, and I watched fascinated as an enamel cup was dipped in, lifted out brimful with dark brown mash, and jars pulled forward and filled in steady rhythm.

Tiny splashes of brown juice dotted my mother's overall as she worked, curls turned to limp black strands across her forehead as clouds of steam from the pot rose to the ceiling.

Pungent smells of hot vinegar, cooked fruit and spices filled the air and followed us out to the back kitchen, as we took the filled jars to cool and decided to have a cup of tea whilst we were waiting.

Sunlight filtered through the small half-opened window on to a wide shelf running the length of the tiny room, each space filled with jars of plum and apple jam, damson, greengage and gooseberry; small bottles with "red-currant jelly" labels, mint, nasturtium,

capers; miniature beetroots in juice the colour
of red wine, pickled cabbage, and brown stone
jars of shallots.

Ma joined us and perched herself on to the
rickety stool opposite, teacup in hand poised
dangerously to one side as she absentmindedly
took sips from it, her whole attention on the
list she had made and which would be fixed on
a nail under the shelf.

"Be thee about, Missus?" a grey head tried
to bob through the half open window, caught
the fly paper across her face and withdrew
smartly.

"Damn and blast they old flies" we heard.
There was shuffling of feet on the cobbles
outside.

"Open the door and come in the proper
way" shouted Ma, putting her list to one side
and reaching for another cup and saucer.

A thin, almost bony woman came in and

stood on the rag mat; in her arms, wrapped untidily in an old woolly jumper, the largest marrow I'd ever seen.

"E'nt thee bin busy?" Zillah's voice was filled with admiration as she placed the bundle carefully down between her feet and took a good look at the nearly filled shelf, and a small sigh of contentment came from my mother at the compliment, filling the silence as we waited to hear the purpose of her visit.

"I could smell thy cookin' right up the path" Zillah went on, bending down and removing the jumper "and I thought if I shared this old feller with thee," she tapped the shiny skin, "p'raps we c'ud both on us 'ave sum o' that luvly marrer ginger."

Ma took her time before answering and I knew what was bothering her; we also had a marrow ripening slowly in the back bedroom and on a shelf in the cupboard beside it a small bottle of brandy, Ma's secret ingredient, making sure of next year's prize in the village show.

Zillah's eyes held a pleading look as she sat hunched up in the chair waiting, and after what seemed ages my mother decided. The yellow mound was lifted on to the table, tapped and with finger and thumb pressed to find out if it was ripe enough and agreed it was.

A few minutes gossip followed, then our friend decided to depart.

"New moon last night" she informed us, getting up and straightening the chair cushion, then with one booted foot on the doorstep and peering up into the blue sky, "S'pose yer turned yer money over and wished?" we were asked.

"We did" Ma answered for us all, anxious for her to go so that we could get our jobs finished.

"Not in front of the winder through glass I 'ope?" "Fraid so" Ma replied trying to hold back her laughter.

"That's dun it" the old girl swung round, her face filled with fear, and throwing her hands up in despair warned "Now Missus thee'll 'ave bad luck for a month," as she returned to the room and stood close to my mother.

"No good thinkin' about they mushrooms we wuz goin' to pick at full moon. Thee've ruined it now by bein' careless. Fancy provokin' they old witches by countin' yer money through glass," she pointed a finger at Ma, "they'll watch it yer dun't pick a single mushroom."

"Witches?" my sister and I said together as Zillah rushed out and slammed the door forgetting her woollie in her haste to be gone.

Ma shook her head, "Old wives tales that's all they are. Let's get back to the kitchen and finish sealing the jars."

Her voice was soothing, and she seemed very sure, but for all that I couldn't help thinking, about those witches, Halloween, pumpkin lanterns, and broomsticks.

On the night of the full moon we three stood outside our front door waiting for Zillah to make an appearance. Ma carried a wide wicker basket over her arm, with a pair of old boots tied to the side of it.

"How much longer do we have to wait?" asked my sister, swinging her paper bag with a big fat pig printed on one side of it and 'Top Quality Meat' written on the other.

As the clock struck ten Zillah walked up the path, black shawled, her skirt held fast round her waist with two rows of sugar string, the hem pinned above her knees with large safety pins revealing long red stockings and galoshes.

The moon for a moment hid behind a thin grey cloud as our friend reached us and stood looking upwards.

"See even 'ee wun't shine proper tonight," her thin arm pointed upwards, her voice filled with gloom. "Reckons I be pushin' me luck comin' with thee – still –." She shrugged her shoulders and led the way and we followed silently to the football field.

Goal posts black-etched guarded a pale yellow patch in the centre of the field, green edged and dew spangled in the moonlight.

"Look at they fairy rings!" Zillah's voice soft with surprise as we saw the dark green circles filled with mushrooms. She sighed and puffed with impatience as Ma tried to unfasten the gate, then we all gave a push and went through.

Boots and galoshes were changed, the women hid their best ones behind the tin shed that had 'Clubhouse' written over the doorway, my sister and I hung ours for safety round our necks by the laces and shuddered as bare feet touched the damp ground.

"Come on Zillah let's go further in by the elms" Ma suggested, as our friend seemed to favour picking close to the gateway. "I be stayin' yer where I be safe" came the reply, "not provokin' they old witches when they be roostin'."

How quiet the night seemed, just the sound of our movement and the faint whispering of water where the small stream curved, and once in the distance from the wood which looked jet black against the hill, a fox barked and seconds later had the call returned.

Soon our baskets were filled with lovely white buttons, pink-lined, and fragile to our clumsy fingers. Then we saw Zillah waving her shawl above her head from the distance like a great bat, warning us it was time to be gone.

The church clock struck the quarter to midnight as Ma slowly walked over to the tin shed, whilst my sister and I sat down by some trees to wipe our feet and put our boots back on.

It was then that we first heard the witches over head, I reckon they must have been flying for a very long time 'cos just between breaths they gave out long sighs and rattled their broomsticks on the branches.

"Ma, witches!" we shrieked, racing across the field. Zillah stood like something turned to stone by the gate, as two owls moved over our heads, circled, and settled on some fence posts.

Boots still unbuttoned, galoshes left behind, our old friend set off for home at a gallop, taking no notice of the mushrooms falling from her basket on to the hard road or the moon shining over her head like a great silver ball, with the 'old man' clearly outlined on it.

"There you are," Ma said brightly as we all stood outside Zillah's house. "We've proved tonight that there's no such thing as spells or wicked witches," but the old woman seemed as though she hadn't heard a word as she bent down and lifted the key from under the flower pot.

"Missus" we heard at last as Zillah opened the front door, and her hand searched in the dark for candle and matches. "I must say thee 'ad some real luck tonight – but thee wudn't 'ave" – her voice triumphant, "only I went up to football field last night 'fore moon got up and left a present in one o' they fairy rings for they old witches."

THIS WAS OUR VILLAGE

Chapter Twenty-Four

GOOD DEEDS

My mother had the 'helping hand' fever really bad this time.

We were used to the steady trickle of people to the door, holding out billycans and asking for them to be filled.

"And a bite to eat, Missus, if you can spare it." Most of these travellers either going to or coming from a night in the workhouse.

Gaunt men came, they were searching for work, medals pinned to their shabby coats, eyes evading yours whilst they awkwardly asked for help, and you couldn't help noticing that one sleeve might be empty, the end tucked into a pocket. Or the limp as they moved down the path, or a round wooden stump where the foot should be showing; men who'd returned from the Great War.

Then the tramps, 'Gentlemen of the road' Ma called them, forever moving from one place to the next, silent and restless, their feet plodding at a steady pace, and only the road ahead interesting them.

There were the 'oddities' that laughed at jokes only heard by themselves or held endless conversations to unseen friends, and the drinkers who threw their whisky bottles on our ash pit as they passed. All knocked on our door and rarely left empty handed.

"Poor things" Ma would say noticing a figure pass the kitchen window just as we sat down to eat, and ignoring our cries of protest she'd snatch one of the dumplings off our plate, heap the last gravy and vegetables from the saucepan and have it warming in the oven almost before the knock came.

Whilst they 'tucked in' to part of our dinner, billycans would be filled and a friendly "good luck" shouted out as they left us.

It was no use telling Ma that they couldn't all be in need, she'd have none of that talk in her house. "Hadn't they kept the Kaiser from our shores and weren't they some mother's son?" and tears would come to her eyes, so we gave up protesting and tried eating meals faster when we saw them coming.

Gypsies came, they found us whilst passing through the village on their way to the Downs.

The women always carried a large woven basket on one arm and either held or dragged along a thin dark-eyed, incredibly dirty child with the other.

In the winter they sold holly or mistletoe, or paper flowers that bore no resemblance in either colour or design to the real thing; perhaps clothes pegs, five inch pieces of skinned down hazel, split through the middle and bound with strips of tin. And when spring time came there'd be primroses and violets arranged in small baskets of woven rushes or grasses.

"Give me a penny, Lady" they'd whine at the door. My mother never had one to spare but she'd go to the kitchen for some food, telling us in loud whispers or signs to keep watch on the plates and cutlery from 'light fingers'. We always did what she asked but they could have taken the lot for we were too frightened to move till she returned.

Good deeds didn't end with the door knocking; we had journeys with soup and rice pudding to young mothers who had somehow

2

contrived to have babies whilst waiting for the wedding day.

Then there were the three weeks with a weeping 'Auntie' in the house who's husband had gone to work one morning, and 'forgot to return', and only when threats of a divorce came from my long-suffering father was a new home found for our unwanted guest.

Even our nights could be shattered with the howlings of a neighbour 'old Rhubarb', a crazy stone deaf man afflicted with 'devils' when the new moon appeared.

"For God's sake give him some of your herb tea" begged Dad after a fruitless hour trying to quieten him. Grumbling, Ma got dressed, filled a jug with something from a bottle standing in the cupboard, picked up a torch and went over to the house.

We heard shoutings and furniture moved at great speed and 'Rhubarb' demanding the devils to "come and fight him in the open like a man." Then my mother's voice, tired and patient, telling him to "drink up like a good lad." There was the sound of broken glass, a thud then silence which lasted the rest of the night and most of next day. I never found out what medicine Ma had given him but whatever it was it certainly had a kick.

I suppose November saw the greatest good-neighbourliness, after someone had started a coal club in the spring, and through the months most of the villagers had managed to save a pound, giving them a ton of coal brought as close as possible to their doors to last out the winter.

On the day it arrived men, women and children would descend like ants to help with the stacking into shed, back kitchen, or out-house.

Such to-ings and fro-ings there were with buckets and wheelbarrows, what shovings and pushings, sweatings and shoutings, before the precious stuff was safely in before dark, the grass swept clean with besoms and the paths swilled down with water.

There were "thanks" and "goodnights" all round then tired, dirty but satisfied we'd done our bit, we'd go home.

It was after one of these evenings when we were on our way up the lane, that a young girl of about nineteen stopped my mother, and pointing to one of the cottages nearby spoke for a long time in a low voice that I couldn't hear.

I caught "Poor old soul, just leave it to me; one of my girls can help out" — Ma was hooked again — I was furious at being kept waiting and having my services given away without being asked, and started to walk slowly up the path.

Ma reached me, breathless with hurrying. "Whatever it is I'm not going" I told her. She stopped dead in her tracks and looked at me, I felt as guilty as sin, "Oh, alright then but only for a week" I promised.

Next morning around eight I stood outside the cottage timidly raising the knocker and letting it go with a bang. There was no reply. I knocked again, a door opened in the next house and an elderly woman in a long black dress covered with a flowing white apron peered out.

"Dun't stand there makin' a noise" she told me irritably, "best get in and up they stairs where she stays now." I drew a deep breath, opened the cottage door and went in.

In front of me on a table stood a very large aspidistra. Only a glimmer of light came from the lattice window showing the highly polished kitchen range laid with wood and coal ready for lighting.

Two tall china dogs, gold-painted chains around their necks, with proud white faces looked down on me from each end of the mantel-piece; a picture of a young girl in a hat with a fine curled feather stood in the centre. I stood admiring the frame, blue velvet edged with silver, when a voice from the top of the tucked away staircase called out, "Come up whoever you are, I'm in here."

I climbed the nine steps in almost total darkness, a smell of cooking cabbage and bacon getting stronger all the way. It was a job keeping my balance at the top as the floor boards sloped sharply away from my feet, then I knocked on the wallpapered door out of politeness and walked in.

A big iron bed with a brass knob on each corner practically filled the room, and lying on it a woman fully dressed, her huge trunk-like legs thrust into slippers too small for them;

stretched to bursting point, the toes turned upwards with the strain.

"So you've come to be my little helper?" I heard from the other end of the bed, I moved my gaze from the legs and looked into a pair of twinkling blue eyes.

"Yes please" I answered, overcome by the friendly voice. She wasn't a bit like the other old people I'd met. Her face was gentle, round and almost unlined, the white hair swathed round her head like a polished hat, there wasn't a hairpin in sight.

She struggled into a sitting position and reached for a leather book half-opened on the bed. I had a quick look round for I could still smell the cabbage and discovered that it came from a cooking pot on an oil stove perched on a chair by her bed.

"That's my dinner" said the woman "soon I'll be putting the pudding on the top, don't you think that's a good way to save oil?"

I wondered when the jobs would be given out but she seemed in no hurry to tell me, but pulling the book close and holding the page down with her finger asked if I'd heard anything about Ruth and Naomi. I told her that I had and that they were "figures from the Bible," having been told all about them at school by Parson only the week before, so it was fresh in my memory.

"We'll get on famously" said the women looking very pleased. "Let's start this morning by reading a passage from the Bible before you get me a bucket of water from the well and put the duster round." Then on Tuesday you can fetch my pension and on Thursday you can spend it!" she laughed quietly at the thought and got me worried.

Surely she didn't mean to give it to me as a present, Ma would play the devil with me for taking a penny from her, and thoughts about refusing whatever she offered popped in and out of my head as the jobs were done.

First a bucket of water from the well, carried upstairs and placed under the wash basin, then the dusting and putting the pudding dish on top of the bacon that was cooking. Finally slipping a rug over the trunk-like legs I said "goodbye," leaving her happy and contented, reading the Bible.

The next day brought the collecting of her pension, it was re-counted by my friend, put into an envelope and stuffed for safety into a jar under the bed. I read the lesson, got on with my jobs and looked forward to Thursday and the big spend.

Thursday morning when I arrived I found a large hessian bag hung over the chair by the oil stove. The money already taken from the jar stood in small piles on an old cigar box beside my old friend's pillow.

"Come on in dear" I was greeted "I'm just about ready for the spending that you're going to do. "Sit here," she patted the bottom of the bed and with eyes sparkling, gave me my first lesson in housekeeping.

"This rent money's for Squire's widow," a finger and thumb pushed a shilling to one side, "and that's for paraffin," a few pence were moved to the edge of the box. "And that pile with the list of prices is for you to pay for the groceries."

"She picked up the two remaining pennies from the box, turned them over in her hand and stroked them then passing them over like a small child, made sure that I wouldn't forget her one luxury.

"Will you ask for white peppermints, double XX's, they're nice and hot and last a long time. Do you know that I can make two last all day my dear, if I'm careful."

328

As I strolled to the village shop swinging the bag in my hand I thought of the ten shillings pension I'd collected earlier, and the old lady's pleasure at being able to save two pence for her one treat of the week. No wonder Ma told me not to be greedy when I asked for more pocket money.

Every Friday morning Squire's widow came to collect the rent and leave a large flat tin plate housing a mouse-sized piece of boiled fish, and whilst she stood there chatting I'd reheat it on the oilstove feeling the humiliation of charity as though it was mine – and said so.

"Bless you, forget it" the old girl couldn't understand my resentment. "I enjoy seeing her, its a bit of company, and as for the fish, well my husband was a catholic and she used to bring it for him, he's been dead and gone some time now but it don't seem as though she's ever noticed."

I visited the cottage daily, doing precious little other than read a passage from the Bible, fetch some water or do the shopping.

She heard my news of school and the Rector's prize I'd won, fingered the black bound prayer book after the prize giving, saw my first pair of shoes, which I wasn't allowed to put on the table in case it brought bad luck; my Girl Guide outfit, and a demonstration of knot tying.

I in turn heard about the daughter she'd lost, the fine son now living in Buckinghamshire and her trust in the Lord who she knew wouldn't let her end her days in the workhouse.

Two years later this son came to fetch her in a very posh car belonging to his employer, our old friend would be staying with him for good we were told, and the young woman who'd spoken to Ma on coal-heaving night and myself saw her off, waving goodbye and blowing kisses till the car was out of sight.

Then we both returned to the cottage and sat down, feeling sad at parting and knowing how much we'd miss her, but after a while the girl sighed, got up and put on a sacking apron. "Come on, let's get movin' on this packin' up" I heard.

THIS WAS OUR VILLAGE

Chapter Twenty-Five

MAY THE BEST MAN WIN

"Who be your Dad votin' for?" I was asked, as a freckle-faced boy with very blue eyes looked down on me from the high wall. Hands came over and gripped the bricks and a ragged jumpered body appeared, a pair of spindly legs decorated with hobnailed boots spattered the gravel at our feet as he swung them over and jumped down.

"Guess 'oo gi'e I this?" a crumpled sheet of paper was pulled from the top of his trousers and unfolded carefully. "Our Cis" we were told, "some bloke in 'er office sez 'ee's an agent."

We crowded round and saw the printed
head and shoulders of a man, and underneath
in bright colours the words:
VOTE FOR LEMMING AND COUNT
YOUR BLESSINGS.

"Ee's the one me Dad's puttin' 'is cross
against" went on Jim, folding the paper back
into its dirty creases. "Saviour of the workin'
classes the agent told our Cis, and we'll all be
better off if 'ee gets in."

"My Mummy's going to vote for Major
Slynne" Leonie's voice beside me was as soft
and silky as the dress she was wearing.

"What! that 'aughty old sod?, our Dad
sez 'ee only comes to see us when 'ee wants
summatt," Jim's scuffed boot kicked the wall
behind him.

"But he's Squire's friend" Leonie replied
importantly.

"I know's all about that" Jim interrupted,

"Squire's widow bin to see our Gran and wants
'er to go and vote at the school next week,
but as our Mam said, the old gal's legs wun't
take 'er. 'Don't worry, I'll send the car for
her', widow promised our Mam 'and John will
collect all the other ladies who can't walk.'

"Gran wusn't arf pleased to 'ear she'd get
a ride. 'Ope me 'and dun't slip wi' all that
excitement' she told 'er, but widder told 'er
she'd only to make a cross, and she was good
enough to tell Gran where to put it."

A dull thudding of horses hooves on hard
chalk road was heard, as a water cart came
slowly towards us, and with a hoarse command
and a pull on the reins, the driver and animal
came to a halt by the village pump.

"Jim, gi'e I a 'and wi this 'oss" shouted
the man, jumping down from his seat and
handing over the reins, "'old 'er steady, boy"
and with "Thee bide quiet, Dimple," he gave

the horse's flank a slap then climbed a couple of steps to reach the pump.

The cap on the top of the barrel-like container on the cart was pulled out and hung on a small chain, swinging gently, then a hose pipe was fixed into position on the pump and the pumping began.

Water splashed in, some missed and trickled down the sides of the cart, ending in a steady stream to feed the long grass at the bank edge.

Soon the job was finished, the cap replaced on top and the boy rewarded for his help with a ride on the cart home.

We ran for a while beside the trotting horse, till the man called to us both "best be gettin' back 'ome."

"See thee on Wednesday," shouted Jim from the back of the horse, "so we can 'ave a bloomin' good shout and get old Lemmin' in."

That evening, outside the shop in the main street, Major Slynne came along to speak to us all. He wore a bowler hat, thick tweed coat and muffler, and walking close to his heels was a thin young man wearing glasses, and with a bag slung over his shoulder crammed full with leaflets.

"Good old Slynney" shouted someone from the crowd. "En 'ee got nice eyes?" a woman asked her friend.

Bowler hat came closer and patted the baby in her arms, "Give me your vote" he pleaded, "and let me help you."

"Well that's more than 'is father duz" came a voice from behind us, there was a scuffle, caps and coats were thrown at our feet and knuckles moved into a punch-up position.

"Vote for Lemming" came a call from the path, and marching along the top of the street

we could see two men holding aloft a huge
banner, followed by youths with slogans across
their caps and children and women pushing
babies in prams.

They clashed head on with our group, men
shouted and fought, the banner was snatched
from hands and trodden on, wives handed
babies over to older girls to mind then rushed
over and tugged at husbands jackets to part
them.

Major Slynne and the thin youth
quietly slipped away, and with us following
on behind, they started to knock on people's
doors.

Ma said not a word when finally he
reached our house; just listened to his patter
and refused the handshake. "Humbugs
everyone of them" she said half to herself as
she went back to the ironing.

Long after the village had settled down for
the night, quarrels and fights almost forgotten,

I sat in bed, knees under my chin, thinking,
and watching the moon come up. Was it true
what Jim had told us that Lemming was the
'Saviour' of the working people, if so that
included us and gosh how we could do with being
richer. I thought of Ma and how last week
we'd seen her cry when my brother told her he
couldn't find work anywhere.

"Don't worry, cut our dinners down" I
suggested, as she wiped her eyes on the corner of
her apron and swore 'twas the pickled onions
close to her that had made them water.

Jim's words came again into my head,
"Thee cum wi' the rest of us to school on
Wednesday and shout." Well, if it would help
Ma I'd be first to start shouting even though
Dad would tan me for being 'common'.

How cold the morning seemed as we ran to
school on Polling Day. It was a holiday for us
as they were using the school classrooms and

ours had the curtains drawn dividing it in half and in the centre on a table stood a large black tin box with a slit on the top. "That's where they bits o' paper be gunna pushed in" said my friend "and see its got a lock so nobody 'ere can open it."

Headmaster came out and asked us what we wanted, he'd a posh blue ribbon pinned on to his breast pocket, shoes polished like mirrors, and wearing his good tempered face as far as I could see.

All his friends seemed in the same mood, only the voters in the queue looked nervous, serious or plainly defiant.

More people rode up on bikes, others walked, two in bath chairs were pushed into school.

Jim's Granny and several old ladies in bonnets and clothes reeking of mothballs, lavender or peppermint were helped from cars, voices were shrill, soft, complaining or sullen, as Squire's friends saw them across the gravel playground.

We kids stood well back from the schoolhouse, ready to run if our audience disliked our chanting.

"Vote, Vote, Vote for good old Lemming," we bellowed, "Chuck old Slynney in the ditch."

Squire's widow gave us a long hard stare as she passed. She'd be telling our mothers so fears mounted and louder came the shouting, then a farmer turned up and each child was given a penny to spend and told what they'd get if they returned.

All day they came in dribs and drabs, there'd never been so many people or cars about, nor so many handclasps, pats on the back, "Good luck" or "May the best man win," the latter said with furtive winks and nods.

Then it was over, the church clock struck nine, black box and strange men departed, Headmaster closed the school, we all went home waiting impatiently till the next day to hear the result of our shouting.

Lemming got in (entirely due to our efforts of course). The nobs were ratty as anything we were told, and Leonie's mother ("silly cat" everyone said) went round for a week wearing a black veil.

Strange, though, we never saw Lemming again, he was busy we heard up in Parliament. Others said "That wi' all they jobs 'e 'ad to do, and speeches 'e 'ad to make — well somehow, 'ee'd got mixed up with 'is promises."

All I know is that Dad had to work just the same, Ma's purse still was empty before the weekend, and we got the same food as we'd had all along; soup, roly-poly or for a change, treacle dumplings.

THIS WAS OUR VILLAGE

Chapter Twenty-Six

PRAYERS AND A PIGLET

"Why are you coming to our church today?" I asked Tilly, as she with her two brothers caught up with me in the lane.

"Our Mam's told us we got to" answered the girl, "so's she can spite old Widder woman 'oo keeps gettin' us jobs down in Somerset wi' they old Nuns wi'out askin' 'er. Our Mam sez she en't goin' to be bossed about like that and she's goin' to send us to whatever church she fancies in future."

The girl sighed and put her arm through mine. "Somerset's a long way off" she said forlornly, "I dun't want our Ted and Nell to go 'cos Mam sez they'll only be getting' eighteen pence a week wages so we wunt' be seein' they very often."

Her mood changed as she noticed the boys scraping the dirt on the edge of the road into small mounds. "'En I told thee a'fore not to muck thee boots" she said angrily, holding on to their jerseys as we went into church.

I slipped into the usual seat but my friends insisted on walking to the top of the aisle, they returned two seconds later like leaves in the wind, being pushed from one pew to the next with angry whispers and gestures from the occupants, finally landing two pews from the bottom to a crowd of us who, with welcoming smiles, allowed them in.

A worse-for-wear bag of sweets was handed round, and we settled down for an hour of instruction.

On the way home I heard, "your 'yms en't as nice as 'ourn, and yer dun't 'ave no scent swung about like we does, nor no pictures." I dared them to show me and it was decided that we would all be taken round that afternoon.

The clock struck two as we presented ourselves at their church, Tilly and her brothers instantly recognised with a beaming smile from the priest. He eyed us with suspicion, which faded a little when, not wishing to repeat the error of our friends in the morning, we sat down quickly in the bottom pew and picked up a prayer book.

Music seemed to be coming from a dim recess in the corner, it was soft, musical, insistent. I heard the swishing of skirts, and a line of small boys in red cassocks and heavily embroidered surplices walked slowly up the aisle.

One carried a long wooden staff topped

with a crucifix of silver, another a small round container on a long chain filled with something sending out wisps of delicately scented smoke as he swung it this way and that.

They reached the altar, bowed and divided into groups, the service began, most of it in a language that I couldn't understand. Voices rose and fell, a single bell tolled, the air seemed filled with sounds and perfume.

Long candles flickered and melted down one side as tiny draughts from the cracks in the windows caught them.

A seated statue of a woman dressed in blue and gold looked down on the dimpled baby in her arms, shadows moved across the crown on her dark painted hair, face, and dress; she looked as though she was smiling and serious, in turn.

My day-dreams came to an abrupt end

with someone kicking my foot and a voice like a muffled fog horn told me "That's the lot," and as we sat nearest to the door we were the first to smell fresh air. Curiosity had been satisfied and only one desire left, to be in to help Dad make the toast for our Sunday tea.

At the top of the hill we met one of our neighbours returning from a walk with her new friend.

He was a pink and white middle-sized pig with short stubby ears and eyes that almost closed when he looked at you, which was often. Dressed in a large blue-ribboned bow tie, he grunted and squealed with delight for Joey seemed to know and trust everyone. There was no reason why he shouldn't for he was petted and fussed by half the village, with a mistress who doted on him, a place in front of the fire, bags of food whenever he squealed. What pig could ask for more?

Once the smallest of a litter and brought into the house for dead, milk and brandy squeezed into his mouth, then wrapped in an old woollen vest and put into a box by the kitchen stove, he was still alive next morning and tenderly looked after, repaying kindness by increasing in size and demands.

We raced with him hard at our heels to the door which was opened almost immediately by a short tough looking man.

"I'ts the oven for 'im soon, Missus" we heard as Joey swaggered past him and stretched himself full length beside the fireplace. "Oh Wilf, don't be so cruel!" came the woman's reply, then the door was shut on the rest of their conversation.

* * * * * *

There must have been a religious revival that winter in our village, what with lantern slides and missionaries, visiting priests and meetings, pamphlets pushed through the letter box, and Lettie, Joey's owner, 'finding the Lord.'

She gave my mother a real pasting with her fervour, running in and out of our house at all hours demanding passages from the Bible to be explained, and I remember her arriving with the Holy Book in the middle of a pastry making session and Ma bolting upstairs! leaving me in her clutches for over an hour.

What she said and how I answered I cannot now recall for I was busy putting things into the oven, and was astonished when I heard myself saying "I'd be delighted to go to chapel the next evening," it must have been her 'sausages for supper' reward that made me so careless with my promises.

Next evening we set out with a lantern for company, hearing many footsteps coming from the blackness and calling out to those we recognised.

"What! out soul savin' Lettie?" came a woman's voice from the direction of the path. "You should be coming with us Nell" my companion told her earnestly. "Dun't thee worry gal, I be goin' somewhere better 'an that." The woman gave a short laugh, and the shaft of light from "The Barley Mow" as she opened the door, guided us for a second along the road.

We trudged on in silence, and turned a bend in the street, coming to the chapel with a single light above the porch.

In front stood a horse drawn caravan and fixed to it a poster lit by a couple of flares, telling us in great red letters "Jesus loves Sinners."

We waited with the crowd that had gathered, 'til a tall man came from the shadows. "Welcome brothers and sisters" he called, stretching out his arms, "Let's go to the Lord." Then leading us he climbed the few steps and into the chapel where we took our coats off and sorted out our seats.

Inside was candlelight, oil lamps, and ferocious heat from a pot bellied stove. My arms touched a table in front of me loaded with instruments. I saw tambourines, mouth organs, several whistles and a triangle; somebody stood holding a piano accordion.

The service started with a man at the harmonium beginning to sing, tambourines were rattled and whistles joined in; we fell on our knees, cried and shouted "Alleluia," got damned and cursed for our sins, forgiven and allowed salvation.

I was given sixpence and kissed on the forehead by a bearded man, the local thatcher, who claimed that he was a "strict tea-tot'ler" and only ever drank cocoa.

Then when it was over we all stood outside in the freezing cold, clasping hands and vowing eternal friendship, though knowing full well that by morning light we'd behave just the same as before the service.

Lettie and I walked home in silence, the supper the last excitement of the day.

On reaching her house the woman looked through the window, shading her eyes to see right into the room. "Wonder where Joey is" she said half to herself, "bet old Wilf's pushed him into the shed to aggravate me."

We went round to find him, the only sound our footsteps on the uneven path. Lettie unhooked the string round a nail driven into the door of the shed, the door swung back slowly and there by the dim light of her lantern were seen a small trough – and swinging above it two pink trotters.

"Joey, my Joey!" Lettie cried out as she put the lantern down and going inside stood looking up at him.

"'Taint no use thee carryin' on" said a voice, for her husband hearing the noise now joined us. "Didn't I tell thee Missus 'fore thee went out that ee'd 'ave to go where all pigs 'is size goes?" he went on angrily. "So let's 'ear no more and come we I indoors and 'ave a bit of supper together."

She stood unmoving for what seemed ages before she turned, then picking up the lantern moved to the door. I closed it and fixed the string back round the nail, and as we passed our house Lettie stopped and took my hand.

"I'm sorry dear I couldn't eat supper tonight," her voice trembled as she held a hankie to her eyes. "Not tonight dear, perhaps some other time." I told her I didn't mind a bit, waited till she'd reached her doorstep then knocked on ours to be let in.

At last, home and safely in bed, I thought of lovable fat Joey, his only crime that he'd outgrown his welcome, and thoughts of him stayed long into the night, then dreams took over, and in them I saw the bearded man bend down and kiss Lettie, heard the woman in the 'Barley Mow' sing a hymn and watched Joey looking up earnestly at the poster with the large red letters saying "Jesus loves Sinners."

THIS WAS OUR VILLAGE

Chapter Twenty-Seven

REMEMBRANCE DAY

"Can I have some money for the school wreath?" I asked my mother, as Pat and I sat playing snakes and ladders after tea.

"Teacher says Headmaster's wife is going to make it for 'Remembrance Day' and it doesn't matter how much we give, 'cos all the poppies used will be paper ones."

Ma didn't answer as she passed us and went upstairs, but I knew she'd heard when the squeaky drawer where she kept the money-box was pulled open, and there was the sound of a key being turned.

"En't no use I askin' our Mam for anythin'," said my friend, shaking the dice and letting it fall, "not after what she told our Gran this mornin.

"En't got two 'apence to rub together." I 'eard 'er say, "not till I gets me widders pension on Friday"."

Next day we practised the hymns at school, and those who had money for the wreath handed it over, then we marched in two lines passed the flagpole and kept saluting, till headmaster decided we wouldn't disgrace him too much.

It was followed by a lecture about cleaning our boots with soot if we hadn't polish, and brushing our hair, and not to sniff or shuffle during the two minutes silence.

Small shafts of sunlight wormed their way between snow clouds as we waited by the schoolhouse on the following Sunday.

Some girls wore black coats, others, black serge dresses with white lacey pinafores, and had their hair tied with wide black ribbons; boys in long black stockings and hobnailed boots, caps, and jerseys with a black arm band sewn on to it.

A whistle was blown as our Headmaster took his place close to the flagpole in the playground, and we stood in a half-circle around him.

His wife brought the wreath out, 'twas a beautiful one, all green leaves and moss round the edges, the centre filled with masses of red poppies; and a black edged card read:

"In Honour of our Glorious Dead, from the teachers and children Church of England School."

Pat and I moved from the front row so that others could see.

"Wonder 'oo's goin' to carry it to cenotaph

this year?" she whispered.

"Well not me that's for certain," I assured her, "'cos nobody in our family got killed going to war."

We were hushed into silence by our teacher giving us a prod from behind, and heard the following announcement.

"As you know, every year we choose a pupil who's lost a relative, to represent the school, carrying our wreath and placing it with the others on the cenotaph; this year it's the girls turn." He paused and patted his tie. "So Patricia, come forward and head the procession."

Pat drew in a large breath, and pushed her way to the top by the open gate, her face flushed, and eyes shining bright as we heard the order "Get into a double line."

A boy was told to stand next to me, in my friend's place. "Can't I march wi' me brother?"

he protested, but 'twas in vain he pleaded; fourteen lines and the cane on Monday was the ultimatum, he hung his head, shuffled, and stood hands in pocket muttering threats to "old 'eadmaster."

We heard "Quick march," Pat led the way through the opened gate and on to the dirt road, followed by infants and their teacher.

Soon it was our turn to go. "Dun't yer stink" said my companion, as boots thudded the ground, as I put a hankie well soaked in eucalyptus over my nose. I just gazed at the Union Jack flying at half mast on the church tower, and made a note in my head to give the boy a sly kick.

On we marched, up the main street past the shops, noticing the large crowd waiting at the cenotaph, and reached it just on time as the fife and drum band finished playing a solemn tune.

Dad was there with lots of other men, all wearing medals; one held a banner with long yellow tassles.

Youths and women with babies in their arms, stood on the high bank to get a better view. Most of them, out of respect wearing mourning, with a scarlet poppy fixed to a peaked cap, or pinned on to a blouse.

Parson gave a short prayer, then we children sung the first verse of "Oh God our help in ages past," and at two minutes to eleven stood with our eyes closed as Headmaster had instructed us, so that nothing would prevent us 'from remembering.'

My 'memories' took me back as far as last night, when Dad had some friends in and we'd crept downstairs to listen to the stories.

There was a place called 'the Somme' where they "went over the top," and we heard how "the Gerries gave them a 'damn good bashing'." [1]

Then Ma opened the kitchen door, standing for a second with her back to us, and she asked if they were ready now for a cup of cocoa, and through the crack in the door I could see Dad polishing his bowler hat with a piece of silk that he kept warming over a candle flame.

Memories ended, I opened my eyes. Parson stood by the cross now, hair and surplice gently blown by the un-warmed breeze, and as he started to read each name on the stone squares a woman close to me burst out "Oh our Charlie."

"Dun't take on so," whispered her husband as he led her away, their footsteps fading long before the roll call had ended.

---

[1] The battle of the Somme, July to November 1916. 58,000 British troops were lost on the first day. Bad weather stopped the Somme offensive on 18 November, by which time the British and French allies had gained just 12 kilometres of ground, and suffered 620,000 casualties. German casualties were estimated to be around 500,000.

'Abide with me' was sung, as the wreaths were placed on the wide grey step; the men, given their order, saluted, small flakes of snow ballet-danced to the ground as Parson closed his book and gave the blessing.

Fifes were silent as the band marched away, only the drums giving out an even beat, behind them followed 'old comrades,' women, children and youths, only a few stayed behind to have a last private look.

Pat and I made quite sure that the wreath wouldn't fall down, then we left.

"Reckon our Dad would 'ave liked they lovely poppies," my friend said slowly, "and I'm bloomin' glad our Mam found they farthins in the button tin, wouldn't seem right to carry wreath out in front if we 'adn't put summat in to pay for it."

THIS WAS OUR VILLAGE

Chapter Twenty-Eight

CELEBRATIONS

An icy wind tore through our clothes and whipped bare legs as we stood peering in the village's largest shop window; whilst several boys, who'd reached there first, waited for the shopkeeper to finish his dinner and open up.

Through a small pane of glass that a heated oil stove had cleared from frost we could see Catherine-wheels displayed on a square board, grey jumping-jacks, squibs and rocket, and around the edge of the board, golden-rain, and roman-candles shaped like a fan in the centre.

We were urged, in black lettering across the feet of an almost life-sized cardboard girl, to "Light your smile with one of our fine sparklers." I counted eight in her stiff hand held high to show her doll-like face, red lips, and a wide set of paper teeth.

"I be 'avin' six of they" said my friend, turning away from the model and unwrapping some money from the end of her woolly scarf. "And two golden-rains and p'raps a pair of roman-candles, 'cos our Mam's given I an extra twopence for me birthday."

"Open the door can't yer" a thin boy shouted through the keyhole, for he'd only a worn blue jersey on, and stockinged feet showed through the hole in the toes of his boots.

He gave a gentle kick to the door and was rewarded by the shopkeeper pointing to a notice and pulling the blind down behind it.

"We open at ONE P.M."

the notice read on the side facing us.

"Let's look at the bonfire while we're waitin," suggested Rachel, so we moved just away from the shop to the long green bank of common ground that stood high from the road in the middle of the village.

A huge cone-shaped pile of wood had been built, almost as high as the bricked wall surrounding young Squire's kitchen garden. Each branch now had ice droplets, hanging down like pearls, and a thick patch of frozen mud fringed the bottom.

"Do you think it will ever burn?" I asked my friend, looking at the frozen mess and thinking how hard everyone had worked; all those barrow loads of brushwood, and handcarts of rubbish we'd brought along, boughs and logs or anything else that could be hauled or dragged.

"Dun't thee worry" Rachel laughed,

taking a stick and prodding the middle of the bonfire, "See that gap? our Jacks gunna fill that 'ole tonight wi' paper balls 'ees 'ad soakin' in paraffin for a week."

A bell ringing up the road reminded us that this was the day for the muffin man and soon he appeared round the corner, stopped ringing the bell whilst he read the shop notice and decided to wait a couple of minutes.

I thought how smart he looked in his navy blue tunic and breeches that reached to his knees, long stockings and black shoes with silver buckles.

On his head was a soft round hat, raised in the centre by a small pad, and balanced on top a tray covered in a green cloth. I told my friend that it was nothing short of magic that it didn't fall off, "P'raps 'ees got it glued on," she answered, laughing.

We heard him speak to the boys and he

was about to turn away when the shop bell gave a clang as the door was opened. In poured the boys, glad to get out of the cold, with pennies in hand ready to purchase.

"Wait your turn!" shouted the shopkeeper, eyebrows twitching like mad under his trilby hat as he struggled with shaking hands to button up his overall.

"Much obliged I'm sure" soothed his wife, taking the muffin tray and after counting the goods handed the tray back to the man with some silver from the till.

He departed, we could shut the door, and it was then that I saw the paper masks hanging on a large rusty nail behind it. There were devil faces painted bright red, Chinamen with tiny beards and yellow tinged cheeks, and black masks thick lipped, with daubs of white paint splashed on.

Rachel and I tried them on, our tongues

moving behind the mouth slits; the smell of glue made the shivers go through my stomach and by the time we'd made our minds up which was the best only sparklers and a few rockets were left to choose from.

Down the road past the shop we opened up the paper bag, once again counting the fireworks. I gave my friend two of mine as a special birthday present.

"E'nt yer kind" she said, stuffing them down her socks, "that's a dozen I got now, and if you'll let I try thy mask for a bit I'll ask Mam if yer can cum to our 'ouse to tea tonight."

Hungry, I ran home for dinner and half way up the path saw Ma busily doing something in the kitchen, then I remembered that as we all sat stoning raisins last night she'd told Dad she wanted to get on with making the Christmas puddings.

"Where have you been?" I was questioned, as a bowl of soup was put in front of me on the overloaded table, and between blowing it cool when Ma wasn't looking and dropping crusts on top, I told her about the fireworks, invitation to Rachel's tea party and the muffin man.

Ma scraped the sugar from the orange and lemon peel and gave me some, then chopped the nuts and put lots of things into the pan she used for jam making. I counted all the basins, read "JAMAICA" out loud from the label on the treacle tin, screwed my mouth and puffed gently on the breadcrumbs scattering them.

What a lovely smell the pint of stout had as it was dribbled into the pan, followed by eggs, sneezy spices and a spoonful of brandy.

"Go outside now and give your hands a jolly good wash" I heard, "then you can stir the pudding and make your Christmas wish."

I returned in time to see her pop in the threepenny-joeys, covering them quickly with flour and suet, then climbed on to a stool, closed my eyes and with her help gave the mixture in the pan a jolly good stir.

I wished (though I didn't say it out loud) for a pair of new shoes with shiny black buttons, but if for some reason I wasn't able to have them a sewing box lined with red silk would be very welcome.

"Hurry up" groaned my sister, "you'll make me late for school." I moved and she stirred like billy-o.

"Our Mam sez that stirring the Christmas pudd's a lot of silly rot" Rachel said, coming to the doorway, but I noticed that she didn't refuse when Ma asked her in and handed her the spoon.

School time seemed endless that afternoon as we sat trying to sew, the pot-bellied stove hardly gave out any heat, and with no windows open – for it was too jolly cold – the walls ran with steam from our breath and trickled to the floor.

At last four o-clock, my friend and I took to our heels, racing across the playground and up the muddy lane, and all the time I was thinking about the birthday tea; would there be ice-cream and jelly with pineapple, followed by fruit cake?

"Tek thee boots off and warm thee feet whilst I 'elps our Mam." Rachel pulled up a stool close to the open fire, and I was left in the company of a large slate-coloured cat who's disdainful green eyes never ceased watching me.

Soft white ashes fell like snowflakes from the grate into a brass fronted box, flickering firelight turned the dresser from golden brown to chocolate. I could hear the even tick of the clock on the mantlepiece, and the murmur of voices behind the closed door.

"Cum on gal, tek thee place close to I near the top" I heard, as a stout woman paddled in carrying plates and a large covered dish.

"Rachel, what 'ave thee dun wi' they best knives and forks for thee friend? And 'urry up do wi' they lumps o' bread."

She sat down and steam-rollered her chair into position, two fat legs curved their way outside the table legs. My friend brought in a cottage loaf split this way and that, together with a lump of butter on a plate, patted into the shape of a rose.

"Let's say grace," two podgy hands tried to cover the double chin, Rachel and I stood and rattled it off like parrots. Her Mum lifted the lid from the willow patterned dish and there, inside, were umpteen pairs of kippers.

How we tucked in and dipped our bread in

the salty fatty gravy. I watched and wiped
my plate dry with a crust as the others did,
and felt jolly glad that Ma wasn't there to
see just what I'd done to my manners.

"Now for the puddin'," the woman
untangled herself and with an effort stood up
and carried out the plates.

"Rachel I'm full" I whispered, "tell your
Mum I can only manage a little bit." "Tell
'er yerself" she answered fiercely, as a large
grey round ball was brought in.

Untying the string the woman swore, as
the steaming hot cloth caught her fingers. I
saw a mass of suet crust erupt across the dish,
followed by a lake of golden syrup.

"Want some more?" I was asked later as
the spoon was dug in and poised over my plate.

"No thank you," I hastily told her.
"Dun't eat enuf to keep a sparrer alive," said
my hostess, giving herself a second helping.

It was long after six o'clock before we'd finished tea and washed up. My friend pulled the curtains back and lifted the lace trimmings. We saw an archway of flickering light halo the narrow end of the church.

"Mam," Rachel shouted from the bottom of the stairs "get thee 'at and coat on quick. Bonfires well alight."

There was no need for a torch to see our way down the lane, and when we turned by the crossroad what a glorious sight; flames stretched long tongues high into the air, veiled now and again by thick black smoke.

Burnt straw and paper floated over our heads, there were tar smells mingled with oil and melting tyres.

"There's our Jack." Rachel's voice rose a notch or two as she noticed that the paraffin bucket was now being used as a stand for the bangers.

"Dun't tell I thee's used all that paraffin on the bloomin' fire?" she yelled at him. "Corze I 'ave" he bawled back, "and sum cart grease old Ted found knockin' about in farmer's yard in an old rusty tin. Cor, Mam, it didn't 'arf go off wi' a wackin' gurt bang."

He came over to us, "Look, singed me cap," he held his face up, bright red and covered with smuts, "and Ted sez its took 'alf me eyebrows."

My friend and I put our masks on and ran in and out of the crowds, "Remember, Remember the Fifth of November," we shouted.

"Why can't they bide quiet for a bit and just look," a fretful voice asked as we passed her for the second time. "Go 'ome if thee dun't like it" Rachel's Mum suggested, "or block yer ears as yer allus duz when farmer calls fer yer rent."

We moved closer to the fire as the damp rose and soaked our feet, then two youths brought along poor old Guy Fawkes, rag hands and feet tied with baling twine to a gate.

Sparks shot up over my head and for a second made a display with golden-rain and roman-candles, then vanished leaving the night sky peppered with stars.

"Well 'ees gone where 'ee wun't come back" we heard as Guy Fawkes disappeared in smoke and cinders.

"Let's get 'ome" Rachel's Mum said, pulling a torch out of her bag and making sure it worked before leaving the bonfire.

The three of us linked arms and got halfway down the road when the woman stopped as though she'd just remembered something.

"Nip back our Rachel and tell Jack that I'll leave 'im two bits of bacon in the oven for 'is supper."

My friend returned and was silent till

we'd reached the lane. "Mam, I thought yer told I this mornin' yer wasn't cookin' that old bacon yet?." "That's right" replied her mother, "but when thee asked for treacle puddin' for thee birthday, me 'ead told I it might be a good idea to put bacon in same pot, and save the firin'."

"Thank you very much for the tea and bringing me home" I told them both, then going in just as Ma handed round hot cups of OXO, I noticed our kitchen was full of delicious smells, and on the table four Christmas puddings.

THIS WAS OUR VILLAGE

Chapter Twenty-Nine

WINTER FROLICS

If summer brought outings winter also had its fun, and with so much talent in the village bursting to come out, what better time than the long dark evenings, when all work out of doors was impossible.

We used to keep a watch on the notices pinned on to the old barn, and one afternoon coming home from school I saw a large printed sheet fixed with four brass drawing pins.

"Smoking Concert Tonight" it said, "Seven o-clock in the Parish Room." I couldn't wait to get home and have my tea before getting ready for the fun.

Long before seven that evening we arrived at the room, to find it nearly filled with men, women and children, everyone jostling for a seat as the unlucky ones would have to stand and be shoved about when the concert started.

There was coughing, clearing of throats and the shuffling noise of feet, women calling their children to order. Young entertainers half dressed in their costumes peeped between the curtains at the audience almost hidden in a thick haze of smoke from clay pipes and 'Woodbines' working at full speed.

A pianist tried to help a lad tune his violin, playing a few notes on the ancient piano, a singer hidden from view reached some top notes, then a few minutes later the curtain was pulled back, revealing a woman seated on a couch. It was our teacher.

She rose gracefully and came to the edge

of the stage, the sequins on the bodice of her long evening dress sparkling as she moved; there were glimpses of thick woollen stockings wedged into black satin shoes, as with a low bow she took her position near the piano.

The opening bars of 'The Old Rustic Bridge By The Mill' was played, and sung in full twice by the singer, who later, with a delicate motion of her hand invited us to join in the chorus.

We did so with great gusto leaving the pianist far behind, there were clappings and foot thumpings as everyone waited for the next item, and children from the audience who were now going to entertain us made a noisy exit to the dressing room.

Someone rushed on to the stage and pulled the curtains tightly together, an anxious voice from the door in front of us asked "Are you dressed yet, Jimmy?" "En't got no trousers

give me yet" came from the same direction,
together with scrapings and groanings.

"Buck up you lot in there" bawled out
the women in the audience, impatient to see
their offspring. There was a loud bang of a
drum at the back of the hall followed by pipes
finally reaching the right note.

"Pig and Whistle" shouted a small boy
as the fife and drum band made their entry,
making a gallant effort to march down the
gangway. It was a bit of a squeeze, people got
up to avoid the drumsticks flailing to left and
right, but at last they reached the bottom of
the room, turning to face us by the stage with
a flourish of music and drumming.

One of the pipers opened the next act by
playing the latest tune "When The Guards
Are On Parade." The rest of the band joined
in as the curtain parted, we saw two rows

of children resplendent in red uniforms who
marched up and down in time to the music,
proudly showing off their tall hats called
'busby's', made from crepe paper and stiffened
with wire.

Every parent stood up and cheered their
own child, the youngsters shouted and waved
back. "Keep marching" they were ordered from
off stage, it was ignored even if the request was
heard, and only the swishing of the curtains
brought an end to the scene.

A local baker came on next, dressed in a
policeman's outfit. He was greeted with loud
groans and impolite suggestions to "buzz off,"
but he smiled at the 'compliment', showing a
row of white teeth.

"I ham going to sing to you" he told us
with confidence. "Well get on wi' it" came a
voice from the back of the room.

'The Laughing Policeman' he announced as though there'd been no interruption. The ditty was started, catcalls smothering the laughs, he decided to stop singing and mimed all the action and about three minutes later, trembling with the effort and wiping his face with a towel was helped off stage and retired to the refreshment room.

There came an interval, for the star turn hadn't arrived. "Can't think what's keepin' 'em" said the woman next to me, her three chins afloat as she wrestled with the problem.

My friend and I went for lemonade and biscuits, spilling the liquid everywhere as we fought to get back to our seats.

"Dun't ferget they glasses and plates" shouted the woman with the warmed-up-vinegar face, coming over to us as we struggled, her hands nervously rolling and unrolling her black apron. "And dun't thee ferget I wants they back 'ole," she added acidly, noticing they were piled high on to the window-sill.

We ignored her for the concert was about to restart. The pianist, refreshed, made trilling noises up and down the keys, somebody pulled at the curtain and six village belles headed by Squire's sister swaggered on to the stage, dressed in top hat and tails, long black stockings and pointed shoes. "Hussies," came a woman's cheerful voice from the back, as they waved their canes and started to sing.

"We Ain't Got A Barrel Of Money" they told us at the top of their voices, six legs kicking high into the air. – "Maybe we're ragged and funny," they kicked again. "But we'll travel the road, sharing our load, Side by side."

There were wolf whistles and shouts, caps thrown on to the stage, frenzied playing by the pianist and more leg kicking. Finally the girls had had enough, one of them tugged at the curtain, a couple of boys darted forward and closed it and the clapping died down.

Then the favourites, Ted and Elsie appeared, they were soon to be married and had arms linked as they crossed over to the lights.

"I'll Be Loving You, Always," came the clear tenor voice of the man, as he looked down into the eyes of the small woman at his side. The audience set up a cheer, he completed the chorus, then they repeated the lines together.

"Good old Ted" shouted the men, women next to them wiped their eyes, a little girl handed Elsie a bouquet, the two artists bowed low and still holding hands made their way from the stage to the wings.

It was nearing ten o'clock, the fifes and drums started to play, we saw the soldiers and the baker, Ted and Elsie, the pianist, our teacher and the six village belles, plus the helpers and the boys who'd pulled back the curtain.

Then we all settled to sing the usual songs 'Land of Hope and Glory' we bawled, 'Clementine', 'I'm for ever Blowing Bubbles' 'Long, Long Trail', and finally 'God save the King.'

There were goodnights, shudders followed by coughing and spitting, as the night air clouted the old men.

"What about they glasses?" came the plaintive call from the refreshment room, but we paid no heed now the twopenn'oth of fun was over, our thoughts were only on getting home, supper and bed.

* * * * * *

Magic lantern nights could always be relied on during the winter, and were held in the big church by Parson.

Earnest young men from the 'Society for the Propagation of the Gospel' showed us how they wooed the natives in 'foreign lands,' whilst we blew on our hands and rubbed one frozen foot against the other in a fruitless effort to keep warm.

We saw slides of coloured people in various stages of undress, clustered around huts of daubed mud and thatched with palm leaves, pigs with laughing faces, eyes all screwed up, babies playing on dirt roads not unlike our own.

One picture of men fishing was shown twice, of them standing up to their waists in the deep blue water, silvery fish flying over the heads of the sunburned natives.

"Cor, I wish that sun wuz 'ere" said a boy at the back of the church, as somebody chose that moment to open the door.

Two lamps were lit and the priest started

to sort out some more slides, we moved out of the pews and walked about to get warm. An older girl gave us one of her 'winter warmers' – a flat khaki-coloured sweet, so hot and tingling that only by hanging your tongue out could you get some relief.

A bell rang, everyone sat down again, oil lamps were put out and the sheet that did duty as a screen straightened.

It was now the turn of the missionaries to show the progress that had been made. The mission station, low colour-washed buildings with tin roofs and a church, now stood at the end of the dirt road, brilliant white in the morning sun, a large wooden cross over the entrance to the doorway.

Priests and natives were shown walking up the aisle, not a naked person in sight, everyone looked solemn, respectful and jolly miserable.

The next slide showed the dispensary with a line of women outside, babies on hips, each with a tiny arm bared, and a priest in a white gown was holding a syringe whilst a mother and her baby nearest to him watched, fear clouding the woman's face. We saw cripples and lepers, old men on rough matting beds, all waiting to be seen.

The last picture of the evening was a blind boy, arms outstretched to the camera, his face with sightless eyes entreating us to look and just above his head hanging on the wall a portrait of a man wearing a robe, with a tract underneath written in red.

A slide with the word FINISHED in bold lettering was shone on to the screen and the first few bars of a hymn was then played on the harmonium.

A large wooden money-box was handed round each pew and I put the penny in Ma had given to me.

We heard the blessing and stood shivering as the lamps were lit again and Parson led the way down the aisle to the open door. "Thank you for coming" he whispered as we passed him and went our way into the frosty night.

On the way home I thought of all the things I'd seen, the palm trees, white church and clinic, the blind boy, and the picture above his head that he couldn't see, Christ's face looking down on him.

*****

Later came threepenny hops, catering for the twelve to twenty year olds; evenings when skill was out and noise in.

We all met in the Parish Hall, boys still at school, farm lads, and bank and office clerks.

The school boys stood in small knots round the billiard table and refused to join in.

389

"Sissy lot!" they jeered to the young gentlemen who were already taking stock of us from the far end of the room, all proudly dressed in dark suits and sporting a tie, patent leather dancing pumps (shoes) and a white silk hankie in their fob pocket.

We'd be lucky if they asked us to dance, they usually brought their own girls along with them; tall willowy blondes and brunettes, with marcelle-waved hair that made you feel seasick, sleeveless dresses of chiffon with fringed hems, and rows of beads round their necks reaching nearly to their knees.

The band on the stage was preparing to start, it had a pianist, learner trumpeter and drummer; the latter would that evening try out his new instrument: a saw, played by drawing a bow across the smooth edge.

A short thickset man walked up and down the dance floor sprinkling french chalk then handed the empty carton to a small boy.

"Now we'll begin with a foxtrot," he waved an arm to the band, and the pianist thumped out the opening bars of 'Somebody stole my gal.'

An office boy got up, bowed and asked a young girl for "the pleasure of a dance," at the same time drawing a silk hankie from his pocket and swinging it delicately into the air.

Placing a firm hand between her shoulder blades with the silk hankie next to her skin, he held her at arms length and started to prance round the room. We got up, girls dancing together, keeping to the edge of the dance floor close to the chairs and missing the elbows of our capering friend by inches.

There were waltzes, valetas, quick steps and Paul-Jones, till the band, hot and perspiring, halted the music and walked off stage. We followed to the refreshment room presided over by our vinegar-faced friend, who had a quick eye for the non-payers of lemonade, and the helpers to two buns instead of one.

Three men dressed in oxford bags and fair-isle pullovers came in, they gave us a dance and were our heroes. Usually they showed us how to do the new steps, tonight I was going to show off mine, it was the 'Charleston', that mad dance of the twenties, taught to me by my forbidden friend.

"Common as mud" my mother called her, I thought she was marvellous, this bold girl with gypsy eyes and an outsize laugh, who showed me how to hold on to the school railings and kick out with each leg in turn.

"Let thee knees go in" she bawled as hers were flung sideways and up to her head. I soon got the hang of this exciting new style of dancing – together with the cane and lines for "vulgar behavior in the playground."

At nine thirty prompt the refreshment lady reappeared and ignoring us started to push the chairs against the wall; it was the signal to go, we trailed to the dressing room for our coats, hanging the pleasure out as long as we could.

Two lights had been switched off by the time we returned, and remarks about "Some on 'em not knowin' wur ther 'omes be" as we stood in the doorway saying our goodnights.

Girls departed in two's and three's, followed by boys in groups calling to us or wolf whistling now and again, and the bandsman with the saw made a few wailing notes on it, before allowing the village to sink into its usual slumber.

THIS WAS OUR VILLAGE

Chapter Thirty

CHRISTMAS CHEER

Snow fell silently on our clothes and boots as we walked down the long drive to the Old Hall shrouded on either side by yew trees and tall creaking elms.

Pale circles of light from the lantern held by my friend showed patches of gravel path quickly turning to white, on this Christmas Eve.

"Let's sing 'Away in a Manger', this time" said a voice, coming from the face and head bound like a mummy in an off-white scarf, as he turned his jacket collar up against the icy wind, pushed hands deep into trouser pockets, jingling the money we'd already collected. "Dun't ferget some of that you be rattlin' belongs to we" he was reminded, as the four of us climbed the broad steps leading to the front door.

Liz hooked the lantern on to the shepherds crook she'd been carrying, and after sniffs, coughs and much feet shuffling we were ready to begin.

With a mighty burst our white-scarfed friend broke into the first line of that well known carol, we joined in and after a mistake or two managed the last few bars singing together.

A light came on above our heads from the ceiling of a porch, the lampshade shaped like a large pink rose. It shone on a heavy nail-studded wooden door, iron hinged and decorated with a round black knocker.

It was opened slowly by a man dressed all in black, our voices faded to nothing at the grand sight behind him.

"Come in please," his invitation was given in a very solemn tone, like Parson when he stood at the graveside. We stood just inside, our wet boots marking the tiled floor.

"I'll fetch the Mistress," the man said and disappeared down a long passage.

During the second or two that we waited I noticed a curved staircase, covered in thick red carpet and held in place with brass stair rods, several coloured paper bells hung from a panelled corner on silver cords, and almost covering one wall a wood carving of St. George dressed in armour and bending down from his horse, sword in hand, and the dragon looking up at him real frightened.

There was a smell of cigar smoke and voices filled with laughter, as a stout man and a lady came out to see us.

"Coo 'en 'ee posh?" our leader sucked a breath in through his teeth, as we noticed the brilliant studs fastening the man's snowy shirt front.

"Would you sing my favourite?" the woman asked, 'Once in Royal David's City,' her voice soft as the velvet ribbon on her long blue gown.

Smoke-weaved patterns floated slowly upwards from the cigar held lazily between plump ringed fingers, as they both stood listening, we gave them all the verses and only stopped when we all ran out of breath.

"Well done," we heard, "that deserves a prize. Shellard are you there?"

The man in black walked in carrying a bowl piled high with fruit together with a smaller one holding lots of silver pieces.

We all said goodbye each clutching an

orange and some silver coins, and feeling bold as we reached the door shouted "Merry Christmas" and as it closed behind us and the porch light went out, counted our blessings by the glimmer of the lantern.

"We're rich, we're rich," shouted the boys dancing around, "we got 'alfcrown's worth I tells yer, a bloomin 'alfcrown."

"So've we" Liz bawled back, then her voice turned sharp as she remembered, "and dun't ferget we all shares that other lot in thee pocket."

Sweets and biscuits for a year with all that money we'd collected, I thought and dreamed of sherbert dabs, liquorice laces, coconut ice and creamy toffee.

"Hey," my friend tugged at my arm, "do you think old shop will still be open? 'cos I've made me mind up to buy Mam and Dad a Christmas present 'fore I puts the rest on some wool fer a new jumper."

We caught up with the boys who were making snowballs and throwing them at each other. Our leader was told to "Piece up the money thee owes we." "Thee 'ang on" he said, trying to wriggle from Liz's firm grasp, "and we'll count it out proper when we gets to old shop where we can see."

Boots crunched along the frozen drive and out on to the village street, the lantern flickered and threw black smoke in our faces, and soon we could see the lamplight through the shop window on rows of bottles, but not any customers.

Our fat friend, aproned, and leaning on his counter surrounded by lard, cheese and bits of bacon, watched with pale red rimmed eyes as we sorted out our money and put four piles of pennies and silver threepenny pieces in a row close to his elbow.

The church clock chimed the quarter twice before we'd decided on our purchases. Liz bought a bottle of ginger beer for her Mum, and five Woodbines cigarettes in a green packet as her Dad's present.

My choice for Dad two packets of pipe cleaners, and Mum, well, she'd get her favourite, a small piece of cheese with green streaks inside it. I remembered the name and asked for gorgonzola. "Best tie that in a sugar bag 'fore it walks 'ome" suggested Liz, as a grubby hand lifted it off the scales and the smell hit us. "Crikey, dun' it pong?" the girl wrinkled her nose, "'nuff to knock I stone dead it bloomin' does."

Once outside the shop we counted the change and fixed it in the top of our socks, then blew the lantern out, for the sky was now clear and everything veiled in a soft light. Only the thatched houses, snow covered, stood out like fat parcels against hedges and trees on the roadside.

"Goodnight and Merry Christmas," we shouted to each other as we parted for home.

I'd got my boots off and drying when Dad came in for supper, and when all the jobs were finished he helped us to put up the decorations; paper chains that we made at school, lanterns and coloured balloons, pieces of holly that dug into your finger, and mistletoe that Dad said you kissed ladies under if you liked them.

It was quite late before we'd finished and two long socks could be found, Ma hung one round each brass bed knob so they wouldn't be missed by our red-coated visitor.

My sister and I jumped into bed and blew out the light, then stayed awake waiting for Christmas.

THIS WAS OUR VILLAGE

Chapter Thirty-One

THE GOODBYES

Time just flew past, soon I'd be fourteen and leaving school; some of my friends had already done so, and found jobs for themselves locally in glove factory, shop, or laundry and one or two into private service.

Only Tilly (my oldest friend) had been provided with work far away. "Old Widow" had decided Taunton in Devon would suit her, and calling on her mother, said the Nuns at the Convent "would train her well in the station that God had already placed her."

Poor old Tilly wept and pleaded but it

wasn't any use. "You knows how I be fixed"
explained her Mum. "I still got all these
litluns and if thee upsets old widder I wun't
get a look in for free coal nor blankets, p'raps,
this comin' winter."

So the day after her birthday my friend
and I set off, carrying a large canvas bag
between us, and said hardly a word as we
walked the turnpike road then turned left
and in a short time reached the station.

Just before the train came in Tilly's mother
bustled up, pushing a pram brimful with crying
infants. "Little varmints," her hand went
down and gave the nearest child a good old slap,
"nearly made I miss sayin' they good-byes."

Steam filled the platform, people poured
out in front of us, porters shouted as goods were
hauled on then found to be wrong and thrown
off again, whilst the guard stood waiting,
very impatient till they'd finished then

blew his whistle, waved a small red flag, and climbed aboard as the train started moving.

"Dun't forget thy new vest if its cold," Tilly's Mum bawled, making the pram and herself keep pace with the girls carriage window, till the gathering speed made her halt by the track and we were left waving to a speck in the distance.

✳ ✳ ✳ ✳ ✳

It was a year later and autumn when we saw her again, Mum and I busy in the garden doing some tidying up and burning, when a voice from the path called out "Want any 'elp, if so gi'e I a rake and lets get started."

It was Tilly, now a slim fifteen year old, dressed in a green skirt that came almost to her ankles and pulled in with a wide belt, a knitted silk jersey edged with blue and cream scallops.

"'Ome for a 'ole week," she replied to Ma's

shouted question, as we both moved slowly towards the path in our mud-clogged boots, "and its the fust 'oliday I've 'ad since leavin' 'ome, so I en't gunna waste a minnit on it."

Ma led the way indoors, bootless and humming a tune, you could hear her bare feet slapping the lino, the kettle was put on, cake tin inspected, and soon we were all sitting round talking.

"Well how are the Nuns?" Ma asked casually as she stirred her tea. Tilly's face for a moment lost its smile. "They be alright I suppose" she answered dully, "I dun't see much on 'em, not wi' all that prayin', only the one as gi'es us our orders and GOD 'ow she keeps us all workin'."

My friend bit her lip, then the words came out with a rush. "Old Widder who got I the job came to see our Mam and Dad, when they old nuns wrote to 'er, sayin I was packin' it in,

and now Mam says she dun't care 'ow 'ome-
sick I be, after a week its back to bloomin' old
Devon."

Ma's face turned a bright pink and
she was about to let forth when the front
door received a mighty wallop, followed by
fluttering sounds and squawks and swear
words from a voice we all recognised.

"Push the door, Gert" I shouted and got
up to give a hand. It was thrown open with
a crash and a bantam flew over my head,
there were "oh"s and "ah"s, and "come 'ere you
brown sod" as hands clutched thin air. "You've
ruined it for laying" Ma said all upset.

Eventually it was caught, held fast and
pushed into a coop, given some corn and a small
pot of water.

"Whatever made you bring it back in an
open basket?" we asked. "It's our Ted's fault"
the girl protested, picking some feathers from

her dress, "Ee told I that damn bird 'ad bin dosed with maize soaked in whisky and wudn't come too for a couple of hours."

Gert stayed for a while to see how the bantam settled down, and sitting there she told us how she'd been six months now at her job in the factory. "I gets a penny a dozen for sewin' thumbs in gloves, and a quarter of an hour for me dinner and the weekends free." She spread out her hands "Well, what more could you want, that's what me Mam said when I told I 'er."

I walked with my friends to the top of the lane, the air fresh and the sky red with a dying sun. "Shepherds delight," we heard as Gert looked up and drew in several deep breaths, "What about bikin' to White Horse Hill in the mornin'?"

"That's alright for thee only we en't got no bikes" Tilly pointed out. "Well bloomin' well cadge some" came the answer.

Prompt next morning at ten o'clock we met by the church, Tilly with an old upright bike borrowed from her mother, I'd wheedled my sister's spanking new racer together with a list of instructions about not going fast, giving free rides and returning it 'as new' to its owner.

Gert seemed to be having trouble with the back tyre on hers, "Our Ted sez 'e reckons its a slow puncture — still it was jolly good on 'im to lend it at such short notice, even if the saddle's nearly fallin' off an' summats wrong wi' one of they pedals."

Our friend straightened up and we both noticed she was wearing a pair of tight navy blue shorts, with red, white and blue braid round the turn-ups, and a bright red sleeveless blouse with tiny anchors in place of buttons, and one strap of her bra hanging down her arm.

"You en't goin' dressed like that?" Tilly's eyes widened with surprise. "Course I be what's wrong wi' it?"

Gert put one slim leg over the crossbar and set off at a pace, we followed well behind till we'd left the village and turned on to the main road.

Mist swirled and left tiny beads of wet on our hair, till we'd climbed the steep hill and the valley was hidden; and came into a blaze of warm sunshine, lark song and a road winding through an avenue of golden beeches.

A pheasant poked its way through a hedge close to our wheels, screeched with fright and showed a radiant set of feathers. "Dun't know 'ow 'ee got left" Gert remarked as we sped on, "'cos our Ted was yer last week wi' they beaters."

Country was left behind, with a tithe barn and muddy tractor yard. Our tyres made hollow sounds on the newly tarmac'ed road which led to a small market town square filled with stalls, and a grey stone statue of King Alfred.

"Let's get a move on" Tilly called out, as we raced one behind the other down a winding street, past the mill where its white powdered mouth spilt out flour into a long row of sacks on a moving belt.

A few miles of hard climbing brought us on to the top of the Downs. Gert stopped and pumped the tyre up for the third time, and was given unwanted advice shouted from some stable lads exercising their horses on the gallops.

"Shut thee row," was her thank you as we remounted our bikes. "Red, white and blue," they sang after us.

"En't tekin' thee out in that fancy dress no more," Tilly warned, as we swung round the bend and came to the crossroads. Then all was forgotten as we saw the White Horse outlined in chalk stretching across the hillside in front of us.

Bikes were pressed into an old rick and covered with straw, bags with food and drink carried between us, and soon we'd walked up the rough track, crossed over to the horse's eye and standing in the centre, made our wish.

Tottle and creamy grass covered the hill to the road below, beyond it soft patches of green and gold, far into the distance the tilled grey-white earth, like a carpet that was worn at the edges.

"Reckon its grub time" said Gert, rubbing the goose-pimples on her arms, as a cool breeze hugging the hillside floated upwards. "Let's sit in that dip on t'other side" suggested Tilly "where they villagers used to dance on feast days, years ago."

Sheltered from the breeze and full of food, we kicked our shoes off and stretched full length on the grass. From the distance I could hear the sound of tinkling bells, then a dog's bark, the sudden thud of hooves and men's voices as they passed into the next field.

"Stop thee mopin'," our short-trousered friend told us both, as she jumped up and started to dance the 'Charleston', we joined in with a few twirls and kicks, then tried another one called the 'black bottom'.

Tilly started singing 'Sheikh of Araby', we followed with 'Desert Song', and tunes from the 'Maid of the Mountains', then Gert made us get in a line and after her tuition, we gave a fine performance of the 'CanCan'.

Breathless and happy we collected our things and walked slowly back down the chalk path. Halfway, Tilly stopped and glanced back up the hill with a rather wistful look on her face.

Straw was brushed from our bikes and the back tyre pressed with finger and thumb. "Ee'll last for a bit but I'll keep me pump 'andy," Gert muttered, then we pushed on our pedals over the crossroads into a small sulky village that had one empty street and every door closed.

Daylight was fading, the valley a sombre grey-mauve, as we hurried on over the open Downs, past the gallops and the burial grounds now owned by rabbits, who pricked up their ears for a second as they caught our sound, then scuttled away into their burrows.

The air gave our bodies a comfortable warmth, as we plunged from the high ground to the old mill, and walked up the winding street back to the town square sprinkled with lamplight.